PERSONNEL

A PRACTICAL HANDBOOK

Sonia Pearson

The Industrial Society

First published in 1994 by
The Industrial Society
Robert Hyde House
48 Bryanston Square
London W1H 7LN
Telephone 0171–262 2401

© The Industrial Society 1994

Revised and reprinted 1997

ISBN 1 85835 0611

**British Library Cataloguing–in–Publication Data.
A catalogue record for this book is available from the
British Library**

Typeset by: Midlands Book Typesetting Company, Loughborough
Printed by: Lavenham Press
Cover design: Integra Communications

The Industrial Society is a registered charity no. 290003

CONTENTS

NOTE TO THE READER

This book deals with many employment issues which are affected by legislation. Readers should bear in mind that the law is changed not only by new statutes but also by decisions of both the British and European Courts and it is important therefore to keep abreast of both new legislation and case law. In case of doubt in any particular case, member companies should check with The Industrial Society's Employment Helpline which provides a free advice service on personnel and employment law matters to companies who are members of The Industrial Society.

Sonia Pearson
June 1997

RECRUITMENT AND SELECTION

Recruitment is one of the core activities of any personnel department. The personnel department has traditionally been regarded as the "hire and fire" department and is still viewed as such by some line managers. It is, of course, a mistaken viewpoint. The personnel department neither hires nor fires anyone – this is the function of line management. The personnel department can, however, make a major contribution to the success of the organisation by ensuring that only suitable candidates of the right calibre are put forward for final selection. The importance of the recruitment function, therefore, should not be underrated.

We will now consider the procedure step by step.

IS A REPLACEMENT NECESSARY?

The first question to be asked when an employee gives notice is whether a replacement is necessary. This is an opportunity to reassess the situation. It is quite possible that the workload has declined since the last incumbent was appointed or the job has radically changed. The job description should be reviewed and any relevant comments made by the employee who is leaving taken into account. The following questions should be considered:

- Has the job content remained constant or has it changed significantly since the last job holder was recruited?

- Has the introduction of technology changed the job in any way?

- Are future company plans likely to affect it in the foreseeable future?

●Should a person with similar experience and qualifications be recruited or should the emphasis be changed?

●Could the job be done by a part–timer?

●Could the work be absorbed by other members of the department?

●Does the position need to be filled at all?

The final decision is a line management one but the personnel department may instigate the enquiry and act as a catalyst or sounding board.

THE REQUISITION

If it is decided to replace the leaver or a new vacancy arises, and the organisation is a medium or large sized one, the next step in the recruitment process is the staff requisition. This is originated by line management and is in effect a "purchase order" for staff. It provides the authority for the personnel department to recruit. Many companies strictly control recruitment and often it has to be authorised by a senior manager or director.

A staff requisition form should contain essential information about the job but should not replace the job specification. The information on the requisition form should include:

●job title

●number of vacancies

●whether it/these are new jobs or replacements

●date required by

●rate of pay

●hours of work

●whether temporary or permanent

●brief description of duties

An example of a staff requisition form is shown on page 21.

DEFINING THE JOB AND PERSON

Before the personnel department can proceed with the recruitment, two further documents are necessary – a job specification and a person specification. These should be drawn up by the line manager. Line managers tend to resist this task and it may be necessary for a member of the personnel department to assist. On no account should they be drawn up by the personnel department alone. Specifying the job and the type of person required is a line management responsibility.

JOB SPECIFICATION

This document describes the essential features of the job and provides the necessary information required by the personnel department in order to start the recruitment process. It is usually set out under the following headings:

●job title

●department/location

●job title of person to whom employee reports

●job titles of subordinates

●hours of work

- grade/salary

- overall purpose of job

- main tasks and responsibilities

- occasional tasks or responsibilities

- principal contacts

- work environment

- any special conditions

An example of a job specification is shown on pages 22–24. Jobs are organic by nature and frequently subject to change. Each time a vacancy arises therefore the job specification should be reviewed.

PERSON SPECIFICATION

The other essential document required before recruitment can commence is the person specification. This describes the type of person required to fill the job. The person specification should be drawn up with reference to the job description and the attributes specified should be strictly related to the job. The following is an example of the type of information required:

- education/qualifications

- experience

- special skills

- personal qualities

- special circumstances

Each of these headings can be further broken down into those attributes which are essential and those which are desirable. Let us consider each of these headings separately.

EDUCATION/QUALIFICATIONS

The level of education and/or qualifications specified should be strictly related to the requirements of the job. Beware of stipulating a higher level than is necessary, particularly under the "essential" column. Care should be taken not to insist on UK examinations or qualifications.

It should be made clear that overseas qualifications of an equivalent level will be acceptable otherwise potentially suitable applicants could be excluded and it could also be regarded as racially discriminatory.

EXPERIENCE

The type, level and length of experience required should be specified. The expression "previous experience" is meaningless on its own as all experience is previous!

SPECIAL SKILLS

There may be some overlap with Education/ Qualifications under this heading but this is not important. What is important is that the essential skills required for the job are recognised and specified. Examples of skills which might be quoted are computer skills or communication skills. Beware of specifying under the essential column skills which can taught in a relatively short time, e.g. specific word-processing skills.

Communication skills and other "people" skills cannot be acquired as easily and to eliminate applicants with all the other required skills on the grounds that they lack a skill which can be easily acquired is counter-productive.

PERSONAL QUALITIES

These are particularly important in jobs which involve contact with the public or where the ability to get on with other people is essential to the performance of the job.

It should be remembered, however, that for some jobs, particularly specialist or creative jobs in, for example, research and development, information technology or design, qualifications, ability or talent may be more important than personality.

SPECIAL CIRCUMSTANCES

Examples of special circumstances may include the ability and willingness to work overtime, to travel, to stay away overnight, to have one's own transport or to be on call.

When completing person specifications care must be taken not to make any stipulations that could be construed as discriminatory on the grounds of sex or race unless they are essential requirements of the job.

It should not be assumed that because a woman is married or has a young family she will not be able to fulfil any of the requirements specified. It is up to her when informed of the requirements to decide whether or not she can meet them.

An example of a person specification is shown on page 25.

INTERNAL ADVERTISING

It is good practice to advertise all vacancies internally, either prior to or at the same time as advertising externally. This ensures that existing staff have at least an equal opportunity of applying for vacancies which interest them as external applicants.

Considerable ill–feeling can be generated if existing employees believe they are not given the opportunity to apply for promotion when suitable vacancies arise or they first learn about a vacancy from a newspaper advertisement.

THE ADVERTISEMENT

A good advertisement should be worded in such a way that it attracts applicants who are suitable for the job. A large response is unnecessarily time-consuming if most of those responding are obviously unsuitable. This situation may, however, be unavoidable in times of recession when people who are desperate for work will apply for any job that is going.

Unless it is contrary to company policy or there are very good reasons for not doing so, the salary should always be quoted in the advertisement as this in itself eliminates many applicants who are either currently earning more than the salary quoted or so much less that they clearly would not be in the running for the job. Would-be applicants have no means of assessing the level of the job if the salary is not quoted.

DISPLAY ADVERTISEMENTS

If a display advertisement is to be used the heading of the advertisement should contain the job title, the salary and the location of the company (if advertising nationally). These should be in bold print in order to catch the eye of any potential applicants and encourage them to read on.

The body of the advertisement should contain a brief description of the job, a brief description of the person required, including the essential requirements of the person specification, followed by the benefits offered and any other attractive features of the job. A well-worded advertisement should enable potential applicants who are suitable for the job to identify with it.

Applicants should be told how to apply e.g. "please telephone for application form" or "please apply in writing enclosing full CV" etc. If there is a closing date for applications, this should be stated.

Take care that the wording of the advertisement does not offend against sex, race or disability discrimination legislation, particularly in the job title and the description of the type of person required. Make sure that the qualifications and experience stipulated can be justified in relation to the job.

CLASSIFIED OR SEMI DISPLAY ADVERTISING

The same principles apply to other types of advertising. If display advertising is not to be used and economy is the main consideration, the wording of the advertisement is equally important. If the advertisement is to appear in a classified section, make sure the job title is the first word of the advertisement. Briefly describe the job, qualifications and/or experience required, rate of pay and how to apply.

Semi-display is a compromise between display and classified styles. It appears under the classified heading in single-column form but provides for a heading in bold print which makes the advertisement stand out.

CHOICE OF MEDIA

The choice of media for external advertising will be determined by knowledge and experience of which newspaper or method of advertising produces the best results for the category of staff to be recruited. If a specialist is required it is helpful to seek advice from those working in the field on the most suitable newspaper or journal to advertise in.

By recording and analysing the source of all applicants for vacancies as they are received a body of knowledge is built up. This can be done by using a Recruitment Progress Form (see page 26). This form is discussed in more detail on page 12.

OTHER SOURCES OF RECRUITMENT

Other sources of recruitment include:

- job centres

- agencies

- head hunters

- recommendations from existing staff

- careers office

- disablement resettlement officer

- local radio

- leaflet drop

- notice boards

- newsagents

Obviously the source used will depend on the level and type of vacancy to be filled.

Job Centres have traditionally been used for the recruitment of manual workers although they handle a much wider variety of jobs. Agencies are widely used for the recruitment of secretarial staff. Head hunters are unlikely to be used for the recruitment of other than the most senior management vacancies.

Recommendations from existing staff are often rewarded by paying an introduction fee to the employee who makes the recommendation, a proportion on engagement and the remainder on the satisfactory completion of a probationary period. Employers should, however, be aware that recruiting by this method may be regarded as discriminatory if it perpetuates the racial balance of the existing workforce.

Local radio may be used where a number of jobs are on offer if it is cost effective. Similarly a leaflet drop is most likely to be used when a recruitment campaign is taking place or when staff are difficult to recruit.

Newsagents' notice boards may be effective for part-time staff as these advertisements are likely to be read by people who are not already in work but might be interested in a part-time job.

EQUAL OPPORTUNITIES

Many companies publish an equal opportunities policy which states that they undertake not to discriminate on the grounds of, for example, sex, race, marital status, religion, age, sexual orientation or disability.

In order to comply with a published Equal Opportunities policy, the recruitment net should be spread widely by advertising in the ethnic minority press and ensuring that people with disabilities are considered fully on their merits. Employers are expected to make reasonable adjustments to meet the needs of disabled persons.

ETHNIC MONITORING

Ethnic monitoring is recommended by the Commission for Racial Equality in its code of practice and many application forms include a question on ethnic origin. This should always be accompanied by an explanation of why the information is required. Alternatively, a separate or tear-off slip, which does not identify the applicant, may be included with the application form. This can be immediately separated from the application form on receipt and used for statistical ethnic monitoring purposes only (see also chapter 5 Records).

It is illegal to discriminate against anyone on the grounds of sex, race, disability or marital status. This applies to all aspects of employment and in recruitment applies specifically to the arrangements made for deciding who is offered employment, the terms offered and refusal to employ. There is no minimum service qualification for bringing a claim of sex, race or disability discrimination. For this reason the application forms of all unsuccessful applicants should be retained with the interview notes for a minimum of three months.

RECRUITMENT PROGRESS FORM

Essential data on incoming applications can be recorded either on computer or by using a Recruitment Progress form (see page 26).

A recruitment progress form has several functions. It:

- records all incoming applications

- analyses the source of all applications

- records the direct costs of recruitment

- provides statistical data

- records the progress of the applicant through the recruitment process

- enables the recruiter to ensure that all unsuccessful applicants have been written to

By keeping the information in this format it is possible to:

- compare the number of application forms returned with those sent out

- compare the number of shortlisted candidates with the total number of applicants

- judge the relative effectiveness of various media by analysing the source of the successful applicants

- calculate the direct costs of recruitment

A recruitment progress form can highlight the fact that whilst one newspaper produces a large response in terms of numbers of applicants, most of the shortlisted candidates come from another source.

This information enables the personnel department to concentrate the advertising in the most effective local or national newspaper or technical or professional journal.

It should not, however, preclude employers from advertising in the ethnic minority press or taking whatever steps are necessary to bring vacancies to the attention of minority groups.

SHORTLISTING

When shortlisting applicants for interview, the application form should be compared with the person specification. Shortlisted applicants should show evidence of possessing the "essential" attributes listed in the person specification.

PREPARING FOR THE INTERVIEW

Interviews should always be conducted in a quiet room free from interruption by people or telephones.

When inviting people for interview the candidate should be given full instructions on how to reach the location, where to park, if appropriate, and also some indication as to how long the interview is likely to last. If the applicant will be required to undergo tests, this should also be stated in the letter.

In the case of candidates travelling long distances, an indication should be given as to what travelling expenses will be reimbursed e.g. rail fare, air fare, petrol costs, etc. This will avoid misunderstandings or arguments when expense claims are presented.

Before the interview commences the interviewer should study the application form or CV in conjunction with the person specification and identify any areas which need investigation. A list of points to be discussed at the interview should then be drawn up.

In order to assess the candidates fairly, a number of questions specifically related to the requirements of the job and the competencies required to carry it out successfully should be drawn up and these should be put to each candidate. However, this method of interviewing should not be allowed to become a straitjacket. Follow-up questions should be put to individual candidates as necessary, to clarify any points arising from the answers given.

CONDUCTING THE INTERVIEW

The main purpose of the interview is for the interviewer to ascertain if the candidate is suitable for the vacancy and for the candidate to determine whether the job is suitable for him or her.

The interviewer should welcome the candidate and explain briefly the form that the interview will take.

Some interviewers at this stage describe the job in some detail. The disadvantage of this is that it enables the candidate to anticipate what the interviewer is looking for and give appropriate answers accordingly.

The interviewer should discuss the employment record of the candidate and ensure that there are no gaps that have not been accounted for. If during the course of the interview gaps are identified, then the reasons for them should be ascertained.

Reasons for leaving previous jobs should be probed. The reason given on the application form may not be the real reason for leaving and careful questioning may uncover facts that are relevant to the applicant's suitability for the vacancy under consideration.

Do not be afraid to ask difficult questions in order to get to the facts but avoid any questions which might be regarded as discriminatory. In particular detailed questions to female applicants on their domestic responsibilities and the arrangements they have made for their children to be looked after should be avoided.

Questions requiring a yes or no answer should also be avoided. The employee should be encouraged to expand the information provided in the application form, not merely confirm it. Questions beginning with what, why, who, when, how, and where are likely to be the most successful in achieving this objective.

In the case of highly specialised jobs it is likely to be the departmental manager who tests the technical or professional knowledge. Evidence of qualifications may be asked for if these are essential for the job.

Notetaking during interviews should be kept to a minimum but important points should be noted. The interviewee is unlikely to object since this is an indication that the interviewer is listening and taking heed of what is said!

At the conclusion of the interview candidates should be given some indication of when they are likely to hear the outcome and whether further interviews are involved.

AFTER THE INTERVIEW

Immediately after the interview, the interviewer should make notes on the applicant's suitability for the job, measuring the applicant against the person specification. It is important not to delay this task. It is difficult to remember all the details of each applicant if the notes are not made until the end of the day and several other people have been interviewed in the meantime.

SECOND INTERVIEWS

It is likely that a second interview with the line manager will take place either on the same day or at some future date. The personnel interviewer should brief the line manager on the information obtained at the first interview, not least because the candidate should not be subjected to a duplicate interview on the second occasion. There may be areas which were not fully explored at the first interview or one or two points which were overlooked and the line manager should be asked to follow these up. The personnel department should not be putting forward at this stage people whom they consider to be unsuitable for the job as this will seriously undermine their credibility.

The objectives of the second interview are:

- to ascertain whether the candidate is acceptable to the line manager

- to ensure that the candidate is technically competent

- to probe any areas of doubt

- to select the most suitable of the shortlisted candidates.

TESTS

Tests, especially psychometric tests, are increasingly used in recruitment to reduce the subjective element of the interview and to ensure that candidates have the necessary skills or personality factors to equip them for the job. When selecting tests to be used in the process of selection ensure that:

- any test to be used is obtained from a reputable source

- personnel staff are properly trained in its use and interpretation

- it is carefully validated on a regular basis

Tests provide useful back-up information and are an aid to selection but they cannot entirely replace the interviewer.

Assessment Centres are sometimes used as a selection method for management. These involve candidates being put through a series of simulated management situations such as an in-tray exercise, a fact-finding exercise, a simulated selling situation or presentation, and being assessed by a panel, which may include line management and/or personnel staff. Before the recruitment process commences the competencies considered necessary for the satisfactory performance of the job to be filled are identified from the job and person specifications and the panel assess the performance and behaviour of the applicants in the simulated exercises against the identified criteria.

If assessment centres are to be used in the selection process either a suitably qualified consultant should be used or staff on the assessment panel should be specially trained in the operation of assessment centre techniques.

THE OFFER

The offer of employment may be made verbally by the line manager or a member of the personnel department (but see Chapter 2 page 27). It should always be confirmed in writing by the personnel department. Details of engagement procedures are contained in Chapter 3.

REJECTING UNSUCCESSFUL APPLICANTS

All applicants should be notified as soon as possible if they have not been successful. Unjustified delay is unfair to the applicant who may be delaying acceptance of other offers of employment in the hope of obtaining that particular job. Not to notify applicants at all that they have been unsuccessful is discourteous and creates a bad impression of the company.

When the number of applicants applying for any one vacancy is overwhelming it may not be possible to reply to individuals personally. If such situations are foreseen a statement may be included in the advertisement that applicants who have not received a reply by a certain date should assume that they have been unsuccessful. Some registered charities adopt this practice as a matter of policy in order to keep their administrative costs as low as possible.

RECRUITMENT POLICY

A published recruitment policy or procedure forms a useful reference document for members of the personnel department, particularly those who have been newly appointed. Personnel policies cover such aspects as:

- who has authority to authorise recruitment
- internal recruitment procedures
- external recruitment procedures
- job and person specifications
- advertising policies and procedures
- equal opportunities policies
- dealing with applications
- payment of expenses
- interviewing procedures
- offers of employment

●medical examinations

●references

●rejecting unsuccessful applicants

The Institute of Personnel and Development has published a Recruitment Code which sets out the standards of conduct to be adopted when recruiting. Some companies have either incorporated this in their own recruitment policies or published codes of conduct based on the IPD Code.

STAFF REQUISITION

To: Personnel Department   Date
From: Dept.
Job Title:
Date required by: No. Required
Is reason for vacancy   ★ Replacement/★New position?
If new position please give name of authorising Manager
Hours of work:
★Permanent/★Temporary (if temporary, state duration)
Salary/rate of pay/grade:
Job and person Specification ★attached/★to follow
To be interviewed by:
Authorising Signature: Date:

★Please delete as appropriate

JOB SPECIFICATION

Job Title: Training Administrator

Department: Personnel and Training Department

Location: Head Office

Reporting to: Training Officer

Responsible for: No subordinates

Hours of Work: 0900–1700 Monday to Friday

Salary: Grade C – £11,000–£14,000 p.a.

Purpose of Job: To provide an effective administrative and support service to the Training Officer

Main duties: Send out joining instructions to management and staff attending internal and external training courses

Book hotel accommodation and arrange travel for delegates attending external courses

Ensure that training room is set up for all internal courses and liaise with course tutors on equipment required

Carry out all administration duties for tutors and delegates on internal courses

Prepare course handouts as required

Ensure that delegates' course assessment forms are returned following attendance at any internal or external course

Job Specification (cont.)

Maintain training records on computer including:

> identified training needs for each individual employee
>
> courses attended or other training completed
>
> training costs

Produce reports for Training Officer at regular intervals as required

Research suitable external courses to meet specific identified needs

Research suitable training venues for residential courses

Check delegates' expenses claims before passing them to Training Officer for authorisation

Answer all queries relating to training administration

Type all Training Officer's correspondence

Write all own letters and other correspondence concerning course bookings, venue bookings, delegates' queries and other training administration matters

Maintain all manual files as required

Job Specification (cont.)

Occasional Tasks: May be required to act as course
administrator on residential courses
(usually two a year – five days each)

Principal Contacts: Course delegates at all levels from
senior management to shop floor;
conference centre managers, hotel
banqueting managers; administration
staff of external training organisations;
course tutors

Work Environment: Shared office with Personnel Officer's
secretary and Records Clerk. Own
computer terminal and word processor

PERSON SPECIFICATION		
	Essential	**Desirable**
Education/Qualifi-cations	GCSE or 'O' level or equivalent English and maths	5 GCSE or 'O' levels or equivalent
Experience	At least 2 years' experience as an administrator or secretary	Training adminis-tration experience
Special Skills	Minimum typing speed 50 wpm Good communication skills Good organiser	Computer and word-processing skills
Personality	Outgoing, able to relate to people at all levels. Self-motivated – prepared to act on own initiative. Cheerful disposition.	Sense of humour
Personal Circumstances	Must be able to stay away from home at least two weeks per year.	Car owner/driver

RECRUITMENT PROGRESS FORM

Vacancy _____ Date Notified _____

Department _____ Required by _____ Closing date _____

Advertisements

Publication _____ Date _____ Cost _____

Publication _____ Date _____ Cost _____

Publication _____ Date _____ Cost _____

Agencies Notified _____

Applicants

Name	Source	Date A/F sent	Date A/F received	Date A/F ack	Date 1st Interview	Date 2nd Interview	Date rejected	Expenses

CONTRACTS OF EMPLOYMENT

Much confusion exists on the whole subject of contracts of employment. There is a common belief that contracts of employment have to be in writing. This is not so. A contract is in existence if there has been:

- an offer

- an acceptance

- a consideration. (The consideration in this case consists of the salary and terms offered in return for the employee being ready, able, and willing to work.)

- the intention to make a legally binding aggreement.

From this it can be seen that if an applicant for a job is made a verbal offer of a job at interview which is accepted for an agreed salary, a contract is in force and can only be broken by the employer giving notice under the contract as if the employee had already started work (in practice the employer will pay in lieu of notice).

TYPES OF CONTRACTS

There are various types of contracts of employment and we will deal with the different features of the main types of contracts and the circumstances in which a particular type of contract should be used.

OPEN-ENDED CONTRACTS

This is the most common type of contract. It is used for "permanent" jobs and is terminable by either party giving to the other the period of notice specified in the contract.

TEMPORARY CONTRACTS

These are usually for a short period to cover a particular contingency e.g. seasonal variations in workload, a temporary replacement for an employee on maternity leave, vacation employment etc. The Employment Rights Act 1996 stipulates that where the employment is not intended to be permanent, the expected duration of the contract must be stated.

The terms and conditions of employment for temporary workers need not be the same as those for permanent employees but such workers must be informed of them in the same way (see "Written Particulars of Terms and Conditions of Employment" below).

It sometimes happens that workers initially engaged on a temporary contract remain on that contract for a long period, their service sometimes exceeding that of several "permanent" employees. Where the terms of employment for temporary employees are less favourable than those for permanent employees this is clearly an injustice and consideration should be given to remedying the situation either by transferring the employees to permanent contracts, unless the employment is likely to come to an end in the near future, or by putting them on the same or broadly similar terms and conditions to permanent employees.

Where an employee initially engaged on a temporary contract is subsequently engaged on a permanent contract, the service is continuous from the original date of joining the company.

FIXED TERM CONTRACTS

Fixed term contracts, as the name implies, have a fixed starting and termination date. The contract automatically ends on the termination date. There is no requirement to give notice.

Terms and conditions for fixed term contracts may be similar to those for contracts of indefinite duration but they do not have to be the same. Although fixed term contracts automatically terminate on a certain date it is important to make provision for the employment to be terminated during the course of the contract by either party giving to the other a specified period of notice. Failure to include such a clause may result in the employer having to pay the employee for the whole of the unexpired term of the contract if the employee is unsatisfactory or the contract has to be terminated prematurely for any reason.

Clauses may be included in a fixed term contract by which the employee waives his or her right to claim redundancy or unfair dismissal in the event of the contract not being renewed on expiry but such clauses may only be included in fixed term contracts of one year or more in the case of unfair dismissal and two years or more in the case of redundancy.

If the contract has been renewed it is the length of the contract at the last renewal date which determines whether such a clause may be included. For example, a two year fixed term contract which contained a waiver clause in respect of unfair dismissal and redundancy could not contain those clauses if it were renewed for only six months.

It should be noted that these waiver clauses apply only in the case of failure to renew the contract on its expiry. If the contract is terminated before its expiry, the employee may be able to claim either unfair dismissal or redundancy, depending on the circumstances, provided he/she has two years' service or more at the time of the termination. If the contract has been renewed, continuity of service is calculated from the commencement date of the first contract.

Fixed term contracts are often used in times of economic uncertainty or planned company reorganisation when it is not known whether the job will continue to exist in the long term. They are also used when funding for a particular post is subject to annual review. They cannot and should not be used as a ploy for avoiding unfair dismissal claims since the waiver clause only applies in the case of failure to renew the contract on its expiry and provides no protection at any other time.

SELF-EMPLOYMENT

The practice of contracting out work or services to people who are self-employed has increased rapidly over recent years. However, the question of whether or not a person is self-employed is not necessarily clear-cut. The fact that an individual undertakes to pay his/her own NI contributions and income tax does not necessarily ensure that that person will be regarded as self-employed by the DSS, the Inland Revenue or an Industrial Tribunal.

If a question arises as to whether a person is an employee or an independent contractor the authorities tend to look at the job as a whole and analyse the relevant factors which would indicate one type of employment or the other.

Some of the factors which would indicate that the person is an employee are:

- the individual receives company sick pay and holiday pay

- the hours of work and degree of supervision are similar to those of other employees

- the individual has no choice as to whether he/she works or not

- the company's grievance and disciplinary procedures apply to the employment

The factors which would indicate genuine self-employment are:

- the individual provides his/her own equipment

- is free to work elsewhere

- fixes his/her own hours of work

- determines his/her own work methods

- is registered for VAT

Self-employed people should be used for short-term projects or specialist work. They should not be used to replace agency "temps" in any capacity. The Inland Revenue would probably take the view that the individual was an employee and that tax and national insurance contributions should therefore be deducted from pay by the employer.

WRITTEN PARTICULARS

One of the reasons for the widespread belief that contracts of employment have to be in writing is the requirement set out in the Employment Rights Act 1996 for written particulars of employment to be given to all employees who have been employed for one month, within two months of their commencing employment. This means that an employee who leaves after one month has the right to request written particulars of his/her employment, even though they do not normally have to be provided until two months after commencement.

Written particulars do not form part of the contract of employment but they are evidence of contractual terms. The information which must be supplied is clearly specified in the Act.

Written particulars must state:

- the names of the employer and employee

- the date when employment began

- the date from which continuous service began

- the scale or rate of remuneration or the method of calculating remuneration

- the intervals at which remuneration is paid (i.e. weekly, monthly etc.)

They must also state any terms and conditions relating to:

- hours of work (including terms and conditions relating to normal working hours)

- holiday entitlement, including public holidays and holiday pay (the information must be sufficient to enable the employee's entitlement, including any entitlement to accrued holiday pay on termination of employment, to be precisely calculated)

- the length of notice which the employee is obliged to give and entitled to receive

- the job title, or a brief description of the work for which the employee is employed

where the employment is not intended to be permanent, the period for which it is expected to continue or, if it is for a fixed term, the date when it is to end

- either the place of work or, where the employee is required or permitted to work at various places, an indication of that and of the address of the employer

incapacity for work due to sickness or injury, including any provision for sick pay, and pensions and pension schemes

any collective agreements which directly affect the terms and conditions of the employment including, where the employer is not a party, the person by whom they were made

where the employee is required to work outside the UK for more than one month:

the period he/she is to work abroad

the currency in which the employee is to be paid

any additional remuneration or benefits

any terms and conditions relating to his/her return to the UK

This statement must be given to the employee before he/she leaves the UK

If the company has 20 or more employees, written particulars must also include a note specifying:

- any disciplinary rules affecting the employee

- a person to whom the employee can apply if he/she is dissatisfied with any disciplinary decision

- a person to whom the employee may apply to seek redress for any grievance arising out of his/her employment and the manner in which such application should be made

If there are no particulars to be entered under any of these headings, this must be stated e.g.

"You are not entitled to any sick pay other than SSP" or "The terms of the company's pension scheme do not apply to your employment"

The Employment Rights Act 1996 stipulates that certain particulars must be contained in one document, known as the principal document. These are marked with a bullet point in the above list.

For details of sickness and absence rules and procedures and pension fund details, reference may be made to other documents. In the case of notice the employer may refer to statutory periods of notice or refer to a collective agreement. However, in the interests of good practice, *all* the main conditions should either be included in one document, or, if they are not, other reference documents, such as the employee handbook, should, wherever possible, be enclosed when the offer of employment is made to the employee (see also chapter on Engagement Procedures).

CHANGES IN TERMS AND CONDITIONS

Any changes in terms and conditions of employment must be notified to the employee in writing within one month of the change. However, this does not mean that terms and conditions can be unilaterally changed by the employer and imposed on the employee. Contracts of employment are subject to mutual agreement and are binding on both parties. Therefore any change in terms or conditions of employment must be agreed with the employee.

Employees do not generally object to an improvement in their terms and conditions but variation of the contract by the employer to the detriment of the employee could result in an action for breach of contract and/or a claim of constructive dismissal.

There is a commonly held belief that contracts of employment can be varied provided the employer gives notice as required under the contract of employment that the change will take place. This is not the case. It is possible under Common Law to terminate the contract by giving due notice and re-engaging the employee on new terms and conditions, but this would not preclude the employer from a claim for unfair dismissal.

It is possible to vary conditions of employment in certain circumstances, e.g. business need, but only after proper consultation. The onus would be on the employer to prove that he had acted reasonably if the employee were to claim constructive dismissal before an industrial tribunal in such cases.

COMPLAINT TO INDUSTRIAL TRIBUNAL

An employee who is not provided with written particulars within two months of joining the company, not notified of changes, or believes the information provided to be incorrect, may complain to an industrial tribunal who will then determine what particulars should have been included or confirm or amend the particulars supplied. There is no penalty for failure to provide the particulars in the required format or to notify changes to the written particulars.

ENGAGEMENT

The engagement procedure starts with the offer of employment and continues until, or possibly beyond, the date of starting. There may be some overlap with induction procedures e.g. a certain amount of administration is necessary on the date of starting which may be included either on the engagement checklist or the induction checklist. Provided the information is covered, it is not really important which checklist it appears on. A rough rule of thumb is that procedures up to the date of starting appear on the engagement checklist and those which occur on or after the date of starting (apart from procedures such as entering data on the computer and passing information to payroll) should be included on the induction checklist.

OFFERS OF EMPLOYMENT

All offers of appointment should be made in writing by the personnel department. Whilst the law requires that employees be provided with details of their contract terms not later than two months after the commencement of employment, best practice requires that they should be contained in or included with the offer of employment so that the employee can make an informed decision on whether to accept the offer or not and any queries or misunderstandings as to the terms and conditions can be resolved before employment commences.

Terms and conditions of employment may be communicated in various ways, e.g:

- By letter only — all terms and conditions are set out in the offer letter.

- By a pre-printed document setting out the terms and conditions of employment accompanied by a brief offer letter.

●By a printed form, obtainable from some
stationers, giving the headings of the information
required, e.g. name, address, job title, details of
pay, holiday entitlement, sick pay entitlement etc.
which is filled in by the employer. This method is
only suitable for very small companies in view of
the amount of manual input required.

●By letter of appointment accompanied by an
employee handbook. The terms applying to the
individual which are required to be included in the
principal document, e.g. name and address, job
title, place of work, salary details etc. are included
in the letter of engagement while conditions
which apply to all employees are contained in the
handbook. Employee handbooks are described later
in this chapter.

Offers of employment are frequently conditional upon:

(a)   receipt of satisfactory references

(b)   a satisfactory medical examination

REFERENCES

In the public sector references are usually taken up prior
to the applicants attending for interview. In the private sector
references are not usually taken up until the offer
of employment has been made and accepted. References
are usually sought from the last two or three employers.
Requests for references should not be made from the
applicant's present employer without the applicant's
consent.

If a standard form is used for obtaining references, the information requested should be of a factual nature. The main aspects which need to be covered are:

- dates of employment

- reason for leaving

- timekeeping/attendance record

- job performance

- honesty and reliability

- whether the company would re-engage

Space should also be provided for general comments.

Beware of asking for information which is not readily available. If too much research is required on the part of the ex-employer, a reply may not be forthcoming at all. On the other hand there is an increasing tendency to ask for detailed information on attendance e.g. "how many days was the employee absent over the past 12 months?" as this provides an accurate picture and is not subjective.

In the case of senior management it is more usual to write a letter giving a brief job description, and the competencies required and asking for comments on the applicant's suitability for the job.

Very often a telephone reference is more valuable than a written one. People are more likely to disclose information about an employee over the telephone that they would not be prepared to commit to paper. If a reference is obtained by telephone, make sure that a note stating the name of the referee, the date of the reference and a brief summary of the facts obtained is made for retention on the employee's file. Some companies have a policy of not providing telephone references so this is not always an option.

It is important to follow up requests for references if a response is not received within a reasonable time. Failure to provide the information required may simply be the result of oversight or the previous employer's inadequate record system but it might be more sinister. Some employers are reluctant to give an unsatisfactory employee a bad reference because they do not want to prevent that person obtaining another job and therefore deliberately choose to ignore the reference request. Unanswered reference requests should therefore be followed up rigorously.

References are given in confidence and the content of an unsatisfactory reference should not be disclosed to the employee. This may cause difficulty if it is necessary to dismiss an employee on account of the receipt of an unsatisfactory reference. However, if the wording in the offer of employment is phrased "this offer is subject to the receipt of references satisfactory to us" or "which we find satisfactory", there is less pressure on the employer to go into details.

MEDICAL EXAMINATIONS

Medical examinations are usually arranged after the individual has accepted the offer of employment. They are normally carried out by the company doctor, if there is one, or a doctor nominated by the company. Occasionally prospective employees are asked to see their own doctor in which case a form stating the information required for the doctor to complete and return must be provided. A fee will be payable in these circumstances. Under the Access to Medical Reports Act the potential employee will have the right to see the report of the medical examination if it is carried out by his/her own doctor.

Alternatively a medical questionnaire may be sent to the prospective employee for completion and return but where this practice is followed, the advice of a medical practioner may be necessary if the information supplied by the potential employee on the completed questionnaire raises doubts as to his or her suitability for the job.

PENSIONS

It is not legal for companies to operate compulsory pension schemes for their employees but if they have an occupational pension scheme it is obviously in their interests to encourage as many people as possible to join. Information on the pension scheme, the rate of contribution and the benefits provided is usually given to new employees at the time of their engagement. Eligibility to join will depend on the rules of the individual scheme but there is usually a minimum service qualification before the employee can join unless he/she is transferring into the scheme from a previous employer's scheme.

Occupational pension schemes may be based on final salary at retirement or they may be money purchase schemes. They may be run by trustees or by an insurance company on behalf of the employer. In either case the initial administration e.g. distributing information and obtaining completed application forms, birth certificates etc. usually falls within the responsibilities of the personnel department.

PRIVATE HEALTH INSURANCE

If the company operates a private health insurance scheme, information on the scheme is usually sent out by the personnel department as part of the engagement procedure. Private health insurance schemes may either be subsidised by the employer or provided free of charge to the employee (although it is a taxable benefit). Employees who join the scheme are usually required to fill in a form giving details of their dependants.

If this benefit is provided under the contract of employment, the wording of the contract should refer to private health insurance and not to any particular provider. This means that the employer can change the provider without having to obtain the consent of each employee. An express clause in the contract reserving the right of the company to change the provider is an additional safeguard.

COMPANY CARS

If the new employee is entitled to a company car, the personnel department may be involved in the initial procedures such as obtaining details of the new employee's choice of car and passing these on to the purchasing department.

Where there is a large number of company car drivers in the organisation there will probably be a written company car policy.

Such a document would set out information such as:

- what the company pays for, e.g. tax, insurance, maintenance etc.

- who pays for petrol for private use

- any restrictions on use of company car e.g.:

  other drivers

  taking the car abroad

  use of car for rallying etc.

- what to do in case of accident

- how to claim car expenses

- what happens if driver is convicted of a motoring offence or loses his/her licence

This document, if it exists, may be sent out as part of the engagement procedure and it may also be necessary to check the new employee's driving licence.

OTHER ENGAGEMENT PROCEDURES

Other engagement procedures may include

- obtaining and issuing security passes

- notifying management, other employees, reception, telephonists etc. of arrival of new employee

- arranging for announcement in company information or news bulletin if appropriate

- ordering or issuing uniform or protective clothing

EMPLOYEE HANDBOOKS

The employee handbook is a professional way of communicating information, not only about terms and conditions of employment but also about the company, its history, philosophy, products and/or services, company rules and benefits, policies and procedures and other aspects which may be of interest to new or existing employees.

A more detailed breakdown could be as follows:

- welcoming statement from the chairman or managing director

- company mission statement

- description of company, its history, products, and organisation

- terms and conditions of employment

- company policies e.g.:

  health and safety

  equal opportunities

  training and development

  retirement

  smoking

  alcohol and drugs

- Company rules e.g.:

  not accepting gifts or inducements

  uniform, protective clothing or dress regulations

  borrowing or removing company property from premises

  health and safety rules

  disclosure of confidential information

  talking to the media

●Company procedures:

sickness/absence notification

accident reporting

maternity procedures

disciplinary procedure

grievance procedure

●Company benefits:

private health insurance

permanent health insurance

medical facilities

welfare counselling

discount purchases

This list is not exhaustive but is an example of the type of information which may be included.

It is advisable that the contractual terms should be in a different section from the non-contractual terms and that it should be made clear in the handbook which terms are contractual and which are not. For example, any policies or procedures which the company may wish to revise or amend in the future should not be included in the contractual section as once they are incorporated into the contract it is extremely difficult to change them. An example of this is the disciplinary procedure. Although reference to the disciplinary procedure must be made in the written particulars, it can be made clear that the disciplinary procedure itself does not form part of the contract of employment.

Employee handbooks may either be bound or looseleaf. The advantage of the looseleaf variety is that it is possible to update individual pages from time to time. However, it is notoriously difficult to ensure that all employees update their own copies and if there is an important change it is advisable to obtain a signature from every employee as proof that he or she has received it. The wording of the handbook should be general in nature and precise details which frequently change should be omitted so that the need to update or amend pages or sections is kept to a minimum.

It is important that employee handbooks should be "user friendly". Large tomes of small print which cover every conceivable situation will never be read. Handbooks should be printed in large print and divided into sections under clear headings so that employees can quickly and easily look up anything they wish to know.

ENGAGEMENT CHECKLIST

Because the engagement procedure is complex, an engagement checklist is a useful reference document to ensure that all procedures are complied with and nothing is overlooked.

Engagement checklists will vary according to the needs of the individual company and its internal procedures. An example of a checklist is given on page 47.

ENGAGEMENT CHECKLIST

Name: .... Date: ....

Job Title: ....

Department ....

ACTION	DATE IMPLEMENTED	
1. Offer letter sent		
2. Formal acceptance received		
3. References: Name of referee a) .... b) .... c)	Requested	Received ....
4. Medical examination		
5. New starter notification to all management/supervision		
6. Birth certificate checked		
7. Driving licence checked		
8. Health insurance form completed		
9. P45, bank details and SSP1L sent to wages		
10. Entered on database		
11. Induction programme arranged		
12. Probationary period completed		

INDUCTION

A good induction programme is vital if a company is to absorb new employees and develop them to their full potential.

The purpose of induction is:

- to make the new employee feel welcome

- to introduce him/her to the company in a structured way

- to encourage the newcomer to identify with the company

- to make the individual an effective employee in the shortest possible time

At the end of a successful induction an employee will:

- know his/her role in the organisation and what is expected of him/her

- feel part of the organisation and the work team

- believe that he/she is making a useful contribution

Companies which have either a poor induction programme or none at all can expect a high turnover of staff in their first few months of employment. This is both costly and inefficient. A good induction programme pays dividends.

Induction programmes should meet both the needs of the company and the individual. Whilst it may be useful, therefore, to have a standard induction programme, which ensures that new employees are given a reasonable introduction to the company, it must be flexible enough to meet the needs of different groups and individuals and it must never be allowed to become stale.

INDUCTION PROGRAMMES

Induction programmes should:

- be planned in advance

- be written down

- define the areas to be covered

- specify the persons to cover each session

- ensure that all those involved have a copy of the programme and are aware of their roles

- provide for both the trainer and new employee to sign that each item has been covered

Ideally a separate induction programme should be drawn up for each new employee jointly by the line manager and personnel officer.

When setting up an induction programme six basic questions need to be asked:

1. What information does the new employee need?

2. Why does he or she need it?

3. When should the information be given?

4. Who is the best person to impart that information?

5. How should the information be imparted?

6. Where should each part of the induction take place?

WHAT DO THEY NEED TO KNOW?

The information new employees need will fall into two categories

- General information about the company, the building and the people to enable the new employee to settle in quickly
- Information about the job itself

The general induction should not be isolated from the job induction – rather the two should go hand in hand. It is important to get the balance right. Information about the company will be similar for most employees, although some will require more in-depth knowledge than others, dependent on their position.

When planning the job induction reference should be made to the job description to ensure that no aspect of the job is overlooked.

WHY DO THEY NEED IT?

Asking the simple question "why" the new employee needs the information focuses the attention on what they need to know and may lead to a rethink on both the content of the programme and how it is tailored.

WHEN SHOULD THEY BE TOLD?

The induction programme should be phased over a period. To attempt to tell new employees everything they need to know on the first day would probably leave them more confused than if they received no induction at all. On the other hand the induction programme should not be too long. People want to start making a useful contribution as soon as possible and an induction that is unnecessarily prolonged or too theoretical may become demotivating in itself. People learn at different speeds and induction programmes should be flexible enough to respond to the needs of the individual.

Remember that once the employee becomes fully established in the job it will be much more difficult to arrange visits to other parts of the organisation or training which involves prolonged periods away from the place of work so every effort should be made to complete the induction programme within the first two or three weeks of starting if possible. Some sessions may have to be delayed however until there are sufficient new starters to make them viable.

WHO SHOULD TELL THEM?

Choose the most appropriate person to carry out each stage of the induction programme. The initial contact is likely to be with the personnel department but the line manager will be responsible for the job induction and also a substantial part of the general induction. In large companies with a highly structured induction others may be involved such as:

- directors or senior managers

- other line managers

- the training officer

- the health and safety officer

These people are likely to be involved in formal sessions involving several new employees, not necessarily as soon as they start. Their involvement is discussed in more detail below.

HOW SHOULD THE INFORMATION BE CONVEYED?

Induction programmes must not be boring. Where formal sessions form part of the programme a variety of training techniques and visual aids should be used. The new employee should be involved as much as possible in the process so questionnaires and quizzes may feature in the programme or employees may be asked to research certain information for themselves.

WHERE SHOULD THE INDUCTION TAKE PLACE?

Wherever possible induction should take place where the action occurs. For example, it is better to take new employees on a tour of the factory than to show them pictures of it.

It is preferable for them to be taken to meet colleagues with whom they will have contact in the future in those colleagues' departments. In this way the work of a particular department can be explained and they can see it in action and meet other members of the department at the same time.

Some companies arrange for employees to experience certain aspects of the work of the company – a spell actually working in a restaurant or accompanying a delivery driver on his rounds provides a real insight into how the company operates at grassroots level and the pressures involved. New employees often enjoy the experience and feel a greater sense of identification with the company as a result.

WELCOMING THE NEW EMPLOYEE

Planning the induction starts as soon as the employee has accepted the job. A letter welcoming new employees to the company, telling them where and to whom to report on the first day, what to bring with them, where to park their cars and giving a broad outline of the first day's programme is a good start to the induction programme.

New employees should be asked to report later than the normal starting time on their first day at work. This will enable the persons receiving them to deal with the immediate crises of the day beforehand so that they can devote their full attention to the new starters when they arrive. It should also reduce the risk of new employees being kept waiting, which is not a good introduction to any company.

THE PERSONNEL ROLE

New starters are usually asked to report to the Personnel Department because there is invariably a certain amount of administrative work to be completed on the first day – collection of the P45 and completion of any necessary forms.

It may be necessary to issue new employees with identity cards or security passes and this will need to be done early in the induction process.

There is also likely to be quite a lot of information to be given or discussed with new employees on their first day relating to their terms and conditions of employment. Do not assume that they have read or will read the employee handbook. Even if they have read it this is a good opportunity to check that they fully understand all the rules and procedures.

The terms and conditions which may require further clarification are:

PAY

- the date on which salaries are normally paid and the method of payment

- how and when overtime is paid if applicable e.g.: with that month or week's salary or the following one

- bonus payments, if applicable

- performance related pay, if applicable

- salary structure and grading

- salary reviews

- an explanation of the payslip

HOLIDAYS

- the dates on which the holiday year begins and ends

- any restrictions on when holiday may be taken

- any shut-down provisions or requirements to take holiday at a particular time e.g. between Christmas and New Year

- the maximum period which may be taken at any one time

- how to book holiday

- the method by which holiday entitlement is accrued

●whether holiday can be carried over from one year to the next

●holiday pay on termination of employment

●what happens if the employee is sick whilst on holiday

●how holiday entitlements apply in the case of shift workers, part-timers who work only two or three days per week, job sharers etc., if applicable

●whether staff are ever expected to work on bank holidays

HOLIDAY PAY

●how holiday pay is calculated e.g.: in the case of manual workers not on single status conditions what payments are included

●payment for working on bank holidays, if applicable

SICKNESS AND OTHER ABSENCE

●the rules for notification of absence – whom to notify and by when

●the rules for self-certification

●the sick pay entitlement and whether it is contractual or discretionary

●what the qualifying days for SSP are in the case of shift workers or other staff who do not work Monday to Friday

●any provision for permanent health insurance

PENSION SCHEME

- if there is an occupational scheme, how to apply for membership

- whether applications have to be made within a certain time

- a brief outline of the main features of the scheme e.g. how pension is calculated, death benefit, widow's/widower's pension etc.

- whether the company will contribute to a personal pension

It is most important that all employees are made fully aware of any financial benefit for which they have to make application e.g. pension or share option schemes. Failure to convey this information might render the company liable for any financial loss suffered by the employee as a result of not being informed of the benefit.

Do not attempt to cover too many subjects on the first day. To bombard new employees with information as soon as they set foot over the door can be counter-productive. However, they do need to be given sufficient information to enable them to operate reasonably effectively and feel confident.

Employees should be informed on their first day of any company rules that might affect them e.g. smoking rules or rules relating to uniform or dress codes, protective clothing or equipment or confidentiality of information. It is embarrassing and demotivating to new employees if they inadvertently break rules that they have not been told about.

NEW STARTER'S PACK

Some companies prepare a special pack for new starters. This may include information about the company, its products and services and organisation. It may also contain the employee handbook and other policies and procedures relevant to the employee plus useful local information e.g. the addresses of local banks, the post office, chemist, supermarket, restaurants, sandwich bars etc. This pack should be given to the employee before leaving the personnel department.

GENERAL INDUCTION

At this stage the employee will, in all probability, be taken to the department in which he/she is to work and the line manager will take over the induction procedure from this point.

The next stage involves:

- introduction to colleagues

- description of the work of the department and how it is organised

- tour of the building

- health and safety regulations

- arrangements for first aid provision

The manager may wish to appoint a staff member to act as mentor to the new employee, answer questions, take him/her to lunch etc.

INTRODUCTIONS TO OTHER STAFF

Initially the introductions should be restricted to people who work in the department and other close colleagues. To attempt to introduce the new employee to everyone in the building on the first day of employment would probably leave the employee feeling overwhelmed and unable to remember anyone. It is better to take the opportunity to introduce the employee to other staff and departments as the need arises so that the meeting is meaningful.

TOUR OF BUILDING AND HEALTH AND SAFETY REGULATIONS

Similarly, if the building is large the initial tour should be restricted to areas which the employee needs to know the location of immediately e.g. lavatories, coffee machines, staff restaurant, fax machine, photocopying equipment etc. Visits to other areas or locations can be arranged later as and when the need arises.

If a later health and safety session is to be arranged it may only be necessary at this stage to inform employees of what to do in case of fire and how to proceed in case of accident, including the location of first aid equipment etc. on the first day.

FORMAL INDUCTION SESSIONS

Formal induction sessions should be slotted into the programme during the first week or two. They should cover:

- company history, products, services and organisation

- company policies and procedures

- company benefits

- health and safety

- visits to other departments or sites

If there are a number of new starters, the sessions may be organised by the personnel or training department.

COMPANY HISTORY, ORGANISATION, SERVICES AND/OR PRODUCTS

This subject should, if possible, take the form of a group session using videos or other visual aids. In times of a normal intake of staff it may be run at regular intervals, say once a month or once every three months when there are sufficient new employees to make it viable. It is probably best if this session is organised by the training department who may wish to draft in directors or senior managers to speak on specific topics.

Some induction programmes include a welcoming speech from the managing director. The problem with this is that business pressures may cause the MD to pull out of the programme at the last minute leaving someone of a much lower status to take his place. This creates a bad impression on the employees who may feel that they are not very highly valued. It is better not to include directors or very senior managers on the programme unless they are personally committed to taking part.

Large companies often have a video which is shown at induction and gives an overall view of the company, its products and/or services, its history and its organisation. Smaller companies who may not have the resources to produce a video of their own may use slides to illustrate different parts of the company and its products.

The opportunity may be taken during this session to show photographs of members of the board. This may enable newcomers to the company to avoid any potentially embarrassing situations caused by a failure to recognise those in high places if they happen to meet them in the corridor or the lift!

Sometimes senior managers may be invited to give a talk on some aspect of the company's business or some recent major achievement – how the company gained a major overseas contract in the teeth of fierce competition, for example, or how the company researched and developed a new product which is currently enjoying a great success. The objective is to instil pride in the company the employees have recently joined. Emphasis should be on genuine achievements – not hype which will soon be seen through and have the opposite effect from that desired.

COMPANY POLICIES AND PROCEDURES

This session may be taken by the personnel or training officer.

Examples of policies which may be discussed are:

- equal opportunities policy

- training and development policy

- maternity policy

- extended leave of absence policy

- alcohol and drug abuse policy

- discipline and grievance procedure

- absence policy and procedures

- any provision for religious holidays, bereavement or compassionate leave, paternity leave, extended leave of absence, territorial army or study leave, if applicable

COMPANY BENEFITS

This session may be combined with the previous one as it should also be taken by the personnel or training officer. Company benefits or "perks" are likely to contribute to the employee's favourable impression of the company so they should certainly feature in the induction process. Examples of company benefits which may be applicable are:

- share option schemes or other profit sharing

- private health insurance

- permanent health insurance

- medical services provided

- medical screening

- mortgage subsidy or loans for house purchase

- company transport

- season ticket loans

- payment of professional subscriptions

- staff shop or discounts on company products

- discounts available from other suppliers

- provision of uniform or clothing allowance

- sports and social clubs

Some companies offer "cafeteria" benefits by which employees select from a number of options those benefits which best meet their needs. Normally such benefits are restricted to a certain value, usually a percentage of salary. In such circumstances employees need to have detailed knowledge of what is on offer so that they can make an informed choice.

If these two sessions are merely treated as an information-giving exercise, they could become boring so every opportunity to use visual aids and encourage participation from delegates should be fully exploited.

If there are several new starters part of these sessions could take the form of a quiz or questionnaire with the new starters researching the information from the employee handbook. This will familiarise them with the contents of the handbook and they are more likely to remember the information if they have had to look it up.

This information needs to be given early in the induction and if there are only one or two starters it may be covered by the personnel department as part of the first day induction.

HEALTH AND SAFETY

The objective of this session is to make the new employees safety-conscious. It is largely a question of attitude training. The session should be run by the health and safety officer, if there is one, or whoever has overall responsibility for health and safety.

Reference should be made to the company's health and safety policy and to the general duties of both the employer and employee as set out in the Health and Safety at Work Etc Act, 1974. Information should also be given on safety committees and safety representatives, if applicable, and on the accident reporting system. The fire procedure should be reiterated.

Health and safety inductions should be relevant to the industry or to the areas in which employees are working. Videos or slides may be used to illustrate particular hazards, especially fire.

If the industry is a hazardous one then clearly attention should be focused on these hazards and on the safety precautions which must be taken. Any rules regarding protective clothing or equipment must be covered in detail.

Employees may be encouraged to participate in the health and safety session by listing potential hazards in the area in which they work (these can be quite extensive even in an office environment) or taking part in a "spot the hazard" competition. This could be organised in any suitable location.

VISITS TO OTHER PARTS OF THE ORGANISATION

A great deal of enthusiasm can be generated by arranging visits for new employees to parts of the business they would not normally come into contact with. A tour of the factory for clerical or secretarial staff especially if they work at head office, can generate a lot of interest and help them to understand the business they are working for.

INDUCTION FOR MANAGERS

The job induction for managers is likely to extend over a longer period than that for more junior staff. They will usually require a greater in-depth knowledge of different aspects of the company's business and will require to meet more people from all over the company.

In cases where new managers are required to meet people in different establishments or different parts of the country, such visits can be combined with specific aspects of the job induction. For example where there are a number of regional offices scattered round the country, each with a sales and operations team, a visit to one regional office could be combined with a study of the operation of the sales department, whilst a visit to another regional office could concentrate on the operations side of the business. Those involved with the job induction should be told clearly what aspects they are to cover to avoid overlap.

A good induction should equip a newly-appointed manager with a broad overview of the company's business and a detailed knowledge of the area in which he/she is to operate.

MANAGEMENT TRAINEES

Management trainees usually require a more in depth induction programme partly because they are new to industry and partly because they do not necessarily know when they are taken on which part of the business they are finally going to work in.

Management training programmes therefore often combine a considerable amount of on the job training in various departments throughout the organisation with visits and other training designed to give them a broad overall view of both the company and the industry in which they are working.

SCHOOL LEAVERS

Special attention should be given to induction programmes for school leavers as they will probably have had little or no experience of industry or commerce and will need help in adapting to the business world. They may take longer to settle in because they not only have to learn about the job but also what is expected of them in the new environment. Account should be taken of this when drawing up the programme which, as always, should be sufficiently adaptable to meet the needs of the individual.

INDUCTION CHECKLIST

An induction checklist should be drawn up listing all the items to be covered, the name of the trainer responsible for covering each item, the date by which it should be completed and a space for the signature of both the trainer and trainee. An example of an induction checklist is shown on pages 67–69.

INDUCTION CHECKLIST

Items to cover	Trainer	Date for completion	Signature and date Trainer	Signature and date Employee
Administration P.45 received NI no. recorded Bank details Personal details form Pension A/F and details Birth/marriage cert. checked (if applicable) Season ticket loans	Pers. Officer ↓	1st morning ↓		

Conditions of
   Employment
Hours of work
  Overtime
  Flexitime
  Meal breaks
Pay
  Dates
  Method
  Payslip
  Salary reviews
Holidays
  Hol. year
  Shutdowns
  How to book
  Timing of hols.
  Hol. pay accrual
  Carry over
  Bank holidays
  Other leave
Sickness/absence
  Notification
  Certification
  Sick pay
  SSP
Notice periods req.
Disciplinary Proc.
Grievance Proc.
	Pers. Officer
	↓
		1st morning
		↓		

Induction Checklist (cont)

Items to cover	Trainer	Date for completion	Signature and date Trainer	Signature and date Employee
Company rules and policies Smoking Passes for goods taken off premises Confidential information Protective clothing	Pers. Officer ↓	1st morning ↓		
Welcome to department Organisation of Dept. Introductions to Supervisor and colleagues	Manager ↓	1st morning		
Function of Dept. Explanation of Induction programme Tour of building to include Cloakrooms/Loos Coffee machines Restaurant First Aid facilities Photocopier Fax machine Notice boards Fire exits	Manager ↓ Supervisor/ collegue ↓	1st day ↓		
Company Induction Description of Company Turnover No. of employees Products and markets Branches Company objectives Future Developments	Director or Senior Manager ↓	Within 4 weeks ↓		
History of Company Company organisation Sales and Marketing	Training Man. Sales Manager	Within 4 weeks Within 4 weeks		

Induction Checklist (cont)

Items to cover	Trainer	Date for completion	Signature and date Trainer	Signature and date Employee
Health and Safety Common hazards Accident prevention Relevant regulations Fire pevention What to do in case of fire Lifting and carrying Protective clothing Accident reporting Safety representatives Fire Officers First aid	Health & Safety Officer	Within 1st 2 weeks		
Company policies and procedures Equal opportunities policy Training and devlelopment policy Maternity policy Absence policy Alcohol and Drugs policy Discipline and Grievance procedures	Personnel Manager	Within 1st 2 weeks		
Company benefits Share option schemes Private health insurance Permanent health insurance Medical services Payment of professional subscriptions Discounts available from other suppliers Sports and social clubs	Personnel Manager	Within 1st 2 weeks		
Visit to factory	Factory Manager	Within 4 weeks		
Validation	Line Manager	End of Programme		

NOTE: The Induction Checklist shown on pages 67–69 is intended as an aide-memoire only. It shows a number of options but these may not be suitable for every organisation. Whilst directors are suggested for certain sessions, and it is very desirable for them to take these sessions if they are available, if frequent inductions take place this may not be possible and it may be more appropriate for a senior manager from the relevant department to conduct these sessions. The timing of sessions is also only one of a number of options and any induction programme must be drawn up to suit the needs of the organisation.

RECORDS

Good records are vital to a well run personnel department. The type of record system used will depend on the size and resources of the company.

Personnel records should not be limited to information about individual employees or information required solely by the personnel department but should also be capable of generating information on a wide range of aspects of human resource management. They should:

- provide an efficient information service to line management

- be capable of a rapid response

- enable the personnel department to make an effective contribution to the business

- enable the personnel department to identify trends

- ensure that the company complies with legislation

It is increasingly important that the personnel department is seen to be making a significant contribution to the success of the business and is not just an expensive overhead.

Whilst reference is made in this chapter to forms, much of the information may well be stored on computer. It is the content of records and their relevance to the business which is important, rather than the method by which records are stored. The following are examples of the types of records and information that may by required.

PERSONAL RECORD

The most important record held in any personnel department is the employee's personal record. This is the basis from which other information is drawn and is indispensable. The basic information required for each individual is:

- name
- address
- telephone number
- date of birth
- date of commencement
- date from which continuous service is calculated
- National Insurance number
- name, address and telephone number of person to contact in case of emergency
- job title
- department
- salary
- dates of job and salary progression in the company

Other information, which may be required and may or may not be recorded separately, is:

- number of dependants (if necessary for company benefits)
- ethnic origin
- qualifications
- membership of professional bodies
- special skills.

WHO NEEDS PERSONNEL INFORMATION?

The personnel department will need to be able to respond to requests for information from:

- line management
- other employers
- government departments
- banks and building societies
- health and safety executive or local authority

The type of information required by these is likely to be:

INFORMATION FOR LINE MANAGEMENT

Information required by line management is likely to include some or all of the following:

- labour turnover statistics
- appraisal records
- individual training and development records
- individual job and salary progression records
- absence statistics
- ethnic monitoring records
- wage and salary information
- disciplinary records of individual employees
- costs of recruitment

LABOUR TURNOVER STATISTICS

For information on this subject see Chapter 6 Leavers.

APPRAISAL RECORDS

These are normally filed in the personnel department. Appraisals are usually conducted on an a minimal basis and may be used for training and development purposes, performance related pay or human resource planning. They may also be relevant in disciplinary cases related to poor performance. The appraisal should have been fully discussed with the appraisee who should have seen and signed the final document. Any correspondence arising out of the appraisal should be filed with it.

TRAINING AND DEVELOPMENT RECORDS

Depending on the size and resources of the company, training and development records may either be held in the personnel department or in the training department. All courses attended and training and development undertaken, in whatever form, should be recorded and filed under the individual's name. The employee may request proof of having attended a certain course at some future date.

INDIVIDUAL JOB AND SALARY PROGRESSION RECORDS

This information will be recorded on the employee's personal record.

ABSENCE STATISTICS

For information on this subject see Chapter 8 Leavers.

ETHNIC MONITORING

The Commission for Racial Equality recommends that ethnic monitoring should be regularly carried out to assess whether equal opportunity is being achieved in the organisation. In order for this to be done effectively the ethnic origin of the individual must be recorded. This is often asked for on the application form or alternatively on a separate or tear-off slip which is kept for monitoring purposes. Keeping the ethnic origin separate from the named individual reduces the risk of racial bias when shortlisting for interview.

However, as ethnic monitoring needs to be carried out in relation to all aspects of employment, e.g. promotion, training and development and also the later stages of the selection procedure, the ethnic origin of the individual will need to be recorded in some way if only to enable his or her progression through the selection procedure and his or her subsequent career to be properly monitored.

When asking for information about ethnic origin it should be explained that this is for monitoring purposes only and will not be misused.

Examples of racial origin include:

- white (this is sometimes separated into British and other European)

- Afro-Caribbean (or African and Caribbean shown separately)

- Asian

- Oriental

●Arabic

●other

Some employers break down the monitoring even further by specifying certain nationalities, particularly if these form a significant part of their workforce, or they may respond to demand by including a category that many of their employees perceive themselves to be in e.g. "black British".

Many people do not perceive themselves as falling into any of the above categories so provision should also be made for "Other – please specify" with sufficient space to enter a possible combination of racial origins.

The most frequently used categories are:

●white

●Afro-Caribbean

●Asian

●other (please specify)

WAGE AND SALARY INFORMATION

Wage and salary information is normally held in the personnel department on individual records and it is usually the personnel department which authorises salary increases. It may also be responsible for notifying employees when a general pay rise has been implemented.

Personnel departments are frequently asked for general information about wage and salary levels either within the organisation or outside. They should be able to provide information on categories of employees by department, section or job title. They should also be aware of any pay anomalies within the organisation and keep abreast of rates of pay in the area.

Details of an employee's salary should not, of course, be disclosed to anyone outside the company without that individual's consent and only disclosed to people in the company who are authorised to have that information e.g. the employee's line manager.

DISCIPLINARY RECORDS

All records of official warnings must be carefully preserved as they will provide vital evidence if the employee is subsequently dismissed and makes a claim for unfair dismissal to an industrial tribunal.

Similarly notes taken at disciplinary hearings and appeal hearings must also be retained as evidence. For further information see chapters 10 and 11 on Discipline and Unfair Dismissal.

COSTS OF RECRUITMENT

All direct costs of recruitment can be obtained from the Recruitment Progress form or its computer equivalent – see page 26.

OTHER EMPLOYERS

The most frequent requirement from other employers is a request for a reference. From time to time the personnel department may also be approached to take part in salary surveys.

REFERENCES FOR FORMER EMPLOYEES

It will considerably ease the provision of references for former employees if the information required is available from one source. This can best be achieved if the manager fills in a termination report when the employee leaves. This report is then filed in the personnel department and can be used for reference purposes as required. An example of a termination report is shown on page 97.

SALARY INFORMATION FOR SURVEYS

Personnel officers are sometimes approached by other employers in the district for salary information for the purpose of conducting a survey. It is useful to take part in exercises of this kind because those who participate usually obtain a copy of the report and this enables the personnel department to keep abreast of what is happening in the area. If the provision of this information presents a lot of difficulty it may be necessary to consider whether the record system could be adapted to provide it more easily.

GOVERNMENT DEPARTMENTS

Government departments may require:

- statistical information on numbers employed

- information on ex–employees who are claiming benefits

Records in the personnel department should be such that statistics relating to numbers employed and the breakdown of the workforce by gender, full-time, part-time employees, etc. can be produced without difficulty. Information on ex-employees who are claiming benefits can usually be obtained from termination reports.

BANKS AND BUILDING SOCIETIES

These usually require confirmation of salary in relation to a mortgage application by an employee. The employee's consent should be obtained in writing before any salary or personal information is disclosed to a third party.

HEALTH AND SAFETY EXECUTIVE OR LOCAL AUTHORITY

REPORTS OF ACCIDENTS OR DANGEROUS OCCURRENCES

If the organisation is not large enough to support its own health and safety officer, it may fall to the personnel department to perform this role. In this case it will be the responsibility of the personnel department to ensure that any accident resulting in "incapacity for work" of three days or more (not including the date of the accident but including any Saturday or Sunday, whether or not these would have been working days) is reported to the relevant authority. This may be either the Health and Safety Executive in the case of a factory or the Local Authority if it is an office.

The reporting of dangerous occurrences i.e. potentially dangerous events, whether they cause injury or not, is likely to be the responsibility of the senior line manager.

Records of accidents and dangerous occurrences must be retained for three years and must include:

- date and time of accident or dangerous occurrence

- full name and occupation of person affected, including nature of injury or other condition

- place where accident/dangerous occurrence happened

- brief description of the circumstances

The Reporting of Injuries, Diseases and Dangerous Occurrences Regulations 1985 (RIDDOR) also require that an Accident Book is kept in a central location and the employer must ensure that all injuries, no matter how minor, are recorded in this book.

An approved form of accident book (BI 510) can be obtained from HMSO. Accident books must be retained for three years from the date of the last entry.

The accident book may not necessarily be held in the personnel department. It may be more appropriate for it to be held elsewhere, especially in the case of a factory where it needs to be easily accessible to the workers.

MANUAL RECORDS

Although most companies now have computerised personnel records or information systems, this does not mean that they can entirely dispense with manual records. Certain documents will always have to be filed manually. These include all documents which require a signature e.g.

- letters of engagement and acceptance

- appraisals

- medical certificates

- disciplinary records

Other documents which will need to be retained in a manual file are those of a confidential nature – references, confidential reports, etc. The Data Protection Act 1984 gave all employees the right to see any information relating to them held on computer. This right of access does not currently apply to manual records, although it will do when the Data Protection Directive comes into force in Oct 1998.

Even if there is a computerised record system in operation, personnel departments still have to handle a large volume of paper. Every job advertisement may result in a flood of application forms or CVs, all of which have to be read and processed. Constant effort is needed to keep all paperwork to a minimum.

Filing cabinets should be weeded regularly. This not only reduces the need to buy additional equipment, thereby effecting a saving on expenditure, but makes it easier to find the really important documents.

DESIGNING FORMS

From time to time it is necessary to design or redesign a form for use in the personnel department. When designing new forms, the following principles should be observed:

- the form should have a good appearance

- it should provide sufficient space to answer each question

- the questions/information requested should be in natural order

- guidance for completion should be provided

- the wording should be clear and precise

- the form should be piloted before being adopted

- it should be on standard sized paper

- it should have a margin for holes if it is to be filed in a ring binder

- it should be kept as simple as possible

- it should have a reference number and date

If forms are changed or redesigned to comply with changes in legislation, the old ones should be disposed of to ensure that they are not used in error.

EVALUATING FORMS

Forms tend to proliferate in personnel departments and often continue to be used when the need for them no longer exists so from time to time all forms and procedures should be scrutinised and subjected to the following questions:

- What is the purpose of this form?

- Why is it necessary?

●Is the process or procedure for which it was designed still relevant?

●What is the worst thing that could happen if it were eliminated?

●How else can its function be performed?

●Is it duplicating information obtained from another source?

●Is each copy really necessary?

If it passes the test, well and good; if it does not, change it or abolish it. Very often procedures continue in existence long after the need for them has passed. Similarly people go on receiving copies of information which they do not really need and which they seldom read. It merely adds to the burden of paperwork accumulating on their desk. Reduce the stress level by reducing the paper — stop sending people information you believe they do not need and see if they notice!

If you are asked for information on a regular basis which is difficult or complicated to obtain, take time to consider whether some kind of system can be set up that will remove the obstacles. Records and information systems must be the servants of the personnel department — not their masters.

LEAVERS

Monitoring leavers is an important function of the personnel department. The level of labour turnover is an indicator of the health of the organisation. Whilst some labour turnover is unavoidable – and indeed healthy – a high labour turnover is an indication of low morale and problems within the organisation which need to be addressed.

An effective personnel department will monitor labour turnover, record reasons for leaving, identify problems and raise these with line management so that remedial action can be taken.

LABOUR TURNOVER

A high labour turnover is both costly and detrimental to the business in terms of efficiency. Before any action is taken to reduce labour turnover it should be measured so that the size of the problem can be fully assessed.

There are standard methods of calculating labour turnover statistics. These enable comparisons to be made with:

- other companies; and/or

- different departments or establishments within the same organisation

If labour turnover figures are produced they should be studied carefully and acted upon. They should be sent to the managers of all the departments featuring in the report and discussed at management meetings. Particular trouble spots can be identified when departments are compared with one another.

Generally speaking labour turnover tends to be highest among low skilled employees. It tends to be considerably lower in the case of skilled or technical staff, management and supervision.

Labour turnover is frequently highest during the first few months of employment. This may indicate inadequacies in induction. Alternatively it may point to the fact that the wrong kind of staff are being recruited, perhaps too highly qualified or experienced for the job they are required to do. If the labour turnover is consistently high in one department it may suggest poor management or supervision.

Often personnel departments are aware of problems in certain departments but cannot convince the management that action needs to be taken to overcome them. Labour turnover figures provide facts on which arguments can be based when making a case.

SEPARATION RATE

The first and most common method of calculating labour turnover is the separation rate. The method of calculating the separation rate is:

$$\frac{\text{Number of leavers in a given period} \times 100}{\text{average number of employees during that period}}$$

The most usual periods over which labour turnover figures are calculated are monthly or quarterly with the annual figure published on a fixed date once a year.

The separation rate on its own does not always give the full picture. A more detailed picture may emerge if it is used in conjunction with the stability rate.

STABILITY RATE

The stability rate is calculated using the following formula:

$$\frac{\text{Number of staff with one year's service or more} \times 100}{\text{number employed one year ago}}$$

Let us take a simple example to illustrate this point.

If there are 9 leavers in a year out of a total of 10 staff in one department, the labour turnover in that department is 900% per annum, which is horrifying.

However, if the stability rate is then calculated it may be found that of the 10 staff on which the measurement was based, nine of them were there a year ago. The conclusion is therefore reached that it is one job in the department that is turning over and the reason for this can be investigated. It may, for example, be one particularly unpleasant or dirty job that keeps turning over, or it may be one manager in the department who can never keep a secretary!

COST OF LABOUR TURNOVER

The full cost of a high labour turnover is rarely appreciated. Apart from the direct costs of replacement, there are a number of less obvious costs which together add up to a formidable sum.

DIRECT COSTS

Examples of direct costs involved are:

- advertising

- agency fees (recruitment)
- agency fees (temporary replacement)
- interview expenses
- overtime working at premium rates
- interviewing time (personnel + line management)
- induction
- training
- administration (secretarial, clerical, payroll, pension fund etc. plus the cost of stationery, postage, etc.)

INDIRECT COSTS

Possible indirect costs are:

- additional supervision of temporary staff
- reduced efficiency
- interruptions to work flow
- loss of production
- higher scrap levels
- higher risk of accidents
- loss of sales
- poor morale
- unsettled longer serving employees
- damage to company's reputation

Not all of these factors apply to every leaver but they are an indication of the issues that may be involved.

If figures relating to costs are attached to each of

these factors the result can send shock waves through the organisation.

It is therefore in the interests of the company to keep labour turnover down to a reasonable level. A nil labour turnover would not be a desirable situation. Every organisation needs a regular input of new blood and new ideas otherwise stagnation sets in. Keeping the balance right is a joint function of line management and personnel. The regular publication of labour turnover statistics is one way of keeping a finger on the pulse of the organisation.

STATUTORY PERIODS OF NOTICE

The Employment Rights Act 1996 sets down minimum periods of notice. These are:

- For the employee:

    one week's notice after one month's service

- For the employer:

    one month but less than two years' service: one week

    thereafter one week per year of service up to a maximum of 12 weeks' notice after 12 years' service.

CONTRACTUAL PERIODS OF NOTICE

The above are minimum periods of notice and do not prevent the employer stipulating longer periods in the contract of employment. Contractual periods of notice which are shorter than those laid down by statute are void. There are still employers whose contracts of employment stipulate one month's notice on either side in the mistaken belief that because an employee is monthly paid, the notice period should also be one month. Employees with five years' service or more are entitled to one additional week's notice for each year of service up to a maximum of 12 weeks as stated above whatever the contract of employment states.

It is advisable to insist that employees give notice in writing to prevent any misunderstandings.

WITHDRAWAL OF NOTICE

If an employee who has given notice subsequently requests to withdraw it, the employer is under no obligation to comply with the request. Once notice to terminate the employment has been given and accepted it is binding on both parties and the notice can only be rescinded if both parties agree.

LONG NOTICE PERIODS

Senior managers sometimes have long periods of notice from the company written into their contracts of employment. This is a form of protection designed to give a certain amount of security should they be dismissed. They are not usually required to work this notice and are therefore entitled to a large sum of money on termination.

Employers sometimes stipulate long periods of notice for all employees but this can be counter-productive. The reason for requiring the long notice period is usually to give the company time to recruit a replacement before the employee leaves, especially in the case of senior staff.

However this rarely happens in practice as the recruitment of a senior manager is a lengthy process.

Employees forced to work long periods of notice against their will are rarely fully committed to the job or the company and they can sometimes be positively disruptive. In such cases the employer may find himself having to pay the employee large sums of money to leave before the notice period has expired. Had the notice period been shorter, this would not have been necessary.

PAY IN LIEU OF NOTICE

If the employer does not wish the leaver to work his/her notice, because, for example, the employee is going to work for a competitor, payment must be made in lieu. This payment must compensate the employee for any loss incurred by not being permitted to work the notice period. Any contractual benefits such as accrued holiday pay should be calculated to the end of the contractual period of notice. Whether the employee who has a company car is entitled to retain it during the notice period will depend on the wording of the contract of employment i.e. whether the right to a company car forms part of the contract or not. If the employee is going immediately to another job with a company car, then there will not normally be a need for the employee to retain the car as he or she will have suffered no detriment by not retaining it

Pay in lieu of notice is usually tax free unless the right to it is an express term in the contract.

EMPLOYEE NOT WORKING NOTICE

If an employee asks to leave before the expiry of the notice period and the employer agrees, no payment is due in lieu of notice as the employee has in effect asked to be released from the contract of employment.

Little can be done in the case of an employee who "walks out", refusing to work the notice period. He or she is not entitled to any payment for the notice period but to sue for breach of contract, as some employers would like to do, would not be productive as one can only sue for damages and it would be difficult to prove loss.

GARDEN LEAVE

"Garden leave" is featuring more frequently in contracts of employment these days, especially in the case of employees who have access to sensitive information which could be useful to a competitor. "Garden leave" combines a long period of notice with a clause stipulating that the employee may not take up other employment without the written consent of the employer. This means in practice that the company can insist that the employee does not take up the new employment until the full notice period has expired and in the meantime the employee is not permitted to come to work. In this way any information that the employee might have acquired in the course of employment will be out of date by the time he/she takes up the new job.

TERMINATION

When an employee gives notice to terminate employment, it is essential that the personnel department is notified as soon as possible. In some companies the personnel department is responsible for notifying the payroll office that employees are leaving and will therefore need information on such matters as how much holiday has been taken in the current year and whether the employee has any outstanding loans to the company, in addition to information relating to the employee's work record and reason for leaving.

In organisations where it is the responsibility of the line manager to notify the payroll that someone is leaving it is possible for employees to leave the company without the knowledge of the personnel department.

To prevent this happening a system must be established to ensure that the personnel department is kept fully informed. An effective method is the termination report which is completed by the line manager and sent to the personnel department as soon as the employee gives notice.

This will provide the essential information required to enable the personnel department to:

- conduct an exit interview

- provide references to other employers

A termination report should contain the following information:

- date of leaving

- date of starting

- reason for leaving

- timekeeping record

- absence record (number of days absent over past year)

- work performance

- conduct

- relationships with supervision/other employees

- whether suitable for re-employment

- remarks

- signature of line manager and date

An example of a termination report is shown on page 97.

REFERENCES

Requests for references should normally be dealt with by the personnel department to avoid the risk of line managers providing references that are inaccurate, untrue or even malicious. References are given in confidence but they must not be malicious or negligent (see also chapter 3 Engagement).

EXIT INTERVIEWS

The purpose of the exit interview is to establish the reason for leaving and to identify any problems so that remedial action may be taken.

Once an employee has given notice an exit interview should be arranged as soon as possible because:

- The chances of obtaining the real reason for leaving are greater if the employee is seen soon after giving notice, particularly if the employee is dissatisfied.

- There is more time to take remedial action to persuade the employee to stay if this is desirable.

Exit interviews may be conducted by line management, by the personnel department, or both. The personnel department may be regarded as more neutral and the employee may be prepared to disclose more information to a personnel officer than to the line manager, especially if the reason for leaving is related to the attitude of the line manager.

If the employee has a grievance then it is important to discuss it as early as possible. The last afternoon of employment after the leaver has received a handsome farewell gift and spent a prolonged lunch hour at the pub is not the most propitious time to get to the root cause of any dissatisfaction.

Reasons for leaving are complex and may require sensitive probing. There may be all kinds of underlying reasons which even the employee may not fully recognise. The employee may tell you, for example, that he is leaving for a better job or she has been offered more money elsewhere. The question to be asked is why they were looking for a better job or more money in the first place. It may be, of course, that these people are highly ambitious with an eye on the main chance wherever they go or they may be professional job-hoppers. On the other hand their leaving may be an indication that the company has failed to provide career progression or has allowed its rates of pay to get out of line with those paid elsewhere in the district or in the industry.

Reasons for leaving should be recorded and may be used as back-up information for identifying problems of high labour turnover in certain areas or certain jobs. They may be coded and broken down into own accord/dismissal and further into avoidable and unavoidable reasons.

TERMINATION QUESTIONNAIRES

Termination questionnaires may replace the exit interview in situations where it is not possible for a member of the personnel department to interview leavers personally. Alternatively they may be sent out to everyone who has left during a certain period e.g. the previous six months, as a type of attitude survey designed to identify the causes of a high labour turnover. In such cases they may be completed anonymously with a pre-paid envelope for return.

They should not replace the exit interview but they may provide truthful answers. If they are completed after employees have left, they have nothing to lose and may be inclined to express views which might not be forthcoming at an interview. An example of a termination questionnaire is shown on pages 98–99.

TERMINATION REPORT

Name of employee: _____

Department: _____

Job title: _____ Date of leaving: _____

Reason for leaving: _____

_____

_____

PLEASE COMMENT ON EMPLOYEE'S:

Timekeeping: _____

_____

_____

Attendance record – State number of days absent over past 12 months

_____

Standard of work: _____

Conduct: _____

_____

Relationships with other employees: _____

Is he/she suitable for re-employment? _____

Remarks: _____

_____

_____

Signed: _____ Date: _____

Job Title: _____ Department: _____

TERMINATION QUESTIONNAIRE

What did you like best about our company?
What did you like least about our company?
What aspects of your job did you enjoy most?
What aspects of your job did you enjoy least?
What do you think of the training you received?
Do you think you received sufficient supervisory support in your job? If not, please comment.
Was there anything that your family/partner disliked about your job?
Why are you leaving the company?

continued overleaf

continued from page 98

Would you recommend the company to a friend?

(Optional)

Name: . . . .

Department: . . . .

Job Title: . . . . Date: . . . .

MATERNITY

The law relating to pregnancy and maternity is complex. For historical reasons the qualifying dates for maternity leave and for statutory maternity pay are different. Industrial tribunals tend to interpret the legal aspects very strictly, not only in relation to the employer, but also the employee. A woman who fails to follow the required notification procedures may forfeit her right to maternity leave and/or statutory maternity pay.

The Trade Union Reform and Employment Rights Act 1993 made significant changes to the law relating to maternity in order to comply with the EC Pregnant Workers' Directive. The Maternity Allowance and Statutory Maternity Pay Regulations 1994 changed the eligibility criteria for statutory maternity pay for the same reason. The new regulations applied to anyone whose expected date of childbirth was on or after the 16th October 1994.

MATERNITY RIGHTS

A woman who is pregnant has the following maternity rights regardless of hours worked or length of service:

- not to be unfairly dismissed because she is pregnant

- time off with pay for antenatal care

- 14 weeks maternity leave

Employees with two years' service or more at the 11th week before the expected week of childbirth (EWC) are entitled to:

- extended maternity leave

Employees with 26 weeks' service at the qualifying week (15th week before the expected week of childbirth) are entitled to:

- statutory maternity pay

UNFAIR DISMISSAL

Under the Employment Rights Act 1996 dismissal of a woman is automatically unfair if it is for any of the following reasons:

- that she is pregnant, or any other reason connected with her pregnancy

- that she has given birth, or any other reason connected with her having given birth

- that she took, or availed herself of, the benefits of maternity leave

- that her contract was terminated within four weeks of the end of her maternity leave when she had provided a medical certificate stating that she would be unfit to work during that period

- that she had the right to be suspended on full pay as a result of having given birth or breastfeeding in accordance with a statute or a Code of Practice issued under the Health & Safety at Work etc. Act 1974 because to continue working might adversely affect the health of herself or the child

- that she had been made redundant and the requirements to offer suitable alternative employment had not been complied with.

No qualifying period of service is required for her to bring a claim before an industrial tribunal if she is dismissed for any of these reasons.

WRITTEN REASONS FOR DISMISSAL

All women who are dismissed while they are pregnant or on maternity leave are automatically entitled to written reasons for dismissal regardless of their length of service. They are not required to ask for them so a system must be set up to ensure that anyone dismissed during pregnancy or maternity leave is sent a letter setting out the reasons for the dismissal.

ANTENATAL CARE

The statutory right to reasonable time off with pay for antenatal care applies to all employees, regardless of their length of service or number of hours worked. The employer may ask to see the appointment card after the first appointment to verify the reason for the requested time off. Pay for antenatal care cannot be offset against contractual sick pay.

14 WEEKS MATERNITY LEAVE

All women are entitled to 14 weeks maternity leave regardless of hours worked or length of service. During this period all their contractual rights, apart from remuneration, are preserved. The leave can commence at any time from the beginning of the 11th week before the expected week of childbirth.

NOTICE OF MATERNITY LEAVE

In order to exercise her right to maternity leave, the employee must give the employer at least 21 days' notice (in writing if the employer requests it):

- of the fact that she is pregnant

- the expected week of childbirth

- the date on which she intends to commence maternity leave

If it is not reasonably practicable to give the 21 days' notice, she must give it as soon as it is reasonably practicable for her to do so.

Whilst the law only requires notice to be given in writing if the employer requests it, it is sensible for the employer to require written notification to prevent any misunderstandings.

The employer has the right to request a certificate from a medical practitioner or registered midwife confirming the expected week of childbirth.

COMMENCEMENT OF MATERNITY LEAVE

Maternity leave will normally commence on the date notified by the employee.

If childbirth occurs before the employee has commenced her maternity leave, the leave commences on the date of childbirth. Childbirth is defined as the birth of a living child or the birth of a child, whether living or dead, after 24 weeks of pregnancy. The employee must notify the employer of the date of birth of the child as soon as is reasonably practicable.

If the employee is absent for a reason connected with her pregnancy after the beginning of the sixth week before the expected week of childbirth, the employer may deem that she has commenced her maternity leave from that date and in that case she will not be able to return to work subsequently even if she is fit to do so. This provision, however, does not have to be observed and can be overridden by a contractual arrangement between the employer and employee that maternity leave will not be triggered in this way

If the employee is absent due to an illness or injury not connected with her pregnancy at the sixth week before the EWC, maternity leave is not triggered and she can continue to receive SSP until she either notifies commencement of her maternity leave or gives birth.

DATE OF RETURN

There is no need for the employee to notify her date of return nor for the employer to seek confirmation of her intention to return. She is automatically entitled to return to the same job at the end of the 14 week period as if she had been granted leave for any other reason.

However, should the employee wish to return to work before the expiry of the 14 week maternity leave period, she must give her employer seven days' notice of her intention to return. If she gives less than seven days' notice, the employer may postpone the date of her return until the seven days have elapsed. The employer may not, however, postpone the date of return beyond the end of the 14 week maternity leave period. If the employer has postponed the date of return but the employee nevertheless returns before the postponed date, the employer is not obliged to pay her for the intervening period.

CONTRACTUAL TERMS

During the 14 week maternity leave period the employee is entitled to all the contractual benefits, other than remuneration, she would have enjoyed had she been at work during this time.

PENSIONS

The full pension rights of a woman on maternity leave must be preserved during any period of *paid* maternity leave. This includes periods when she is in receipt of SMP.

In the case of a contributory pension scheme, the employee's contributions are pro-ratad to her maternity pay e.g. if the employee contribution is 4%, she will pay 4% of SMP or her contractual maternity pay.

As the pension benefits must be based on her normal salary the employer's pension fund will be required to fund the difference.

EXTENDED MATERNITY LEAVE

Women with two years' service or more at the 11th week before the expected week of childbirth are entitled to extended maternity leave.

In order to qualify for this right a woman must:

•still be employed i.e. have a valid contract of employment, whether or not she is actually at work, at the 11th week before the EWC

•have complied with the notification requirements outlined above under the 14 weeks maternity leave heading and in addition indicated her intention to return

Extended maternity leave includes the 14 week period of maternity leave and can commence any time from the beginning of the 11th week before the EWC.

The employee must return within 29 weeks from the beginning of the actual week of childbirth.

WRITTEN CONFIRMATION OF INTENTION TO RETURN

In the case of women entitled to extended maternity leave, the employer may write to the employee not earlier than 21 days before the end of the 14 week maternity leave period to seek confirmation that she still intends to return. The employee must reply within 14 days unless it is not reasonably practicable for her to do so or she may lose her right to return. The letter from the employer must clearly state the possible consequences of failure to reply in the time required.

This option for the employer should be exercised with some discretion. If the letter is automatically sent out 21 days before the end of the 14 week maternity leave period, women who commenced their maternity leave at the 11th week before the EWC may not yet have given birth and will probably not be in a position to make a rational decision as to whether they still wish to exercise their right to return. Since the law decrees that the letter may be sent "not earlier than" 21 days before the end of the maternity leave period, it would be sensible to wait until a few weeks after the birth.

NOTIFIED DATE OF RETURN

The employee must notify her employer in writing of the date she intends to return at least 21 days in advance.

The employee may postpone her notified date of return for up to four weeks for certified medical reasons connected with her health – not the baby's. This right can be exercised once only and the four weeks cannot be extended for any reason – even if the notified date of return was earlier than 29 weeks from the date of childbirth. If she is unable to resume work at the end of the four week period, she loses her statutory right to return.

The employer may postpone the date of return for up to four weeks provided the reason for the postponement is given to the employee. The employer is not required to pay the employee during this period.

REFUSAL TO ALLOW EMPLOYEE TO RETURN

If an employer fails to allow the employee to return to work on her notified date of return she will be treated as dismissed and if the reason is on account of her pregnancy or maternity leave, the dismissal will be automatically unfair.

RIGHT TO RETURN TO SAME JOB

The job to which the employee is entitled to return is the one in which she was employed before she went on maternity leave, on terms and conditions not less favourable than those which would have been applicable to her if she had not been absent. If there has been a pay increase or improvement in conditions while she has been on maternity leave, the new pay and conditions should apply to her employment on her return.

If the original job is no longer available, e.g. because of a genuine redundancy situation she must be offered suitable alternative employment if this is available. In order to be deemed "suitable", the terms and conditions must not be substantially less favourable than those she enjoyed under the previous contract. If there is no other suitable employment then the reason for her dismissal will be redundancy and she will be entitled to redundancy pay. Failure to offer her suitable alternative employment if it is available would render the dismissal automatically unfair.

CONTINUOUS EMPLOYMENT

Provided that the employee returns to work within 29 weeks from the beginning of the week of childbirth, or at the end of her contractual maternity leave period if this is longer (see the following pages), her service will be continuous from the original date of joining the company.

PART-TIME EMPLOYMENT

Many employees returning to work after maternity leave wish to work part time. The statutory right to return does not extend to the right to return to the same job on a part-time basis, although she has the right to ask for this.

The employer has a duty to consider whether the job could be done part time (possibly on a job share basis) and if this is genuinely not possible, whether other suitable employment exists which could be offered to the employee. Failure to consider these alternatives might lead to a claim of indirect sex discrimination. In such cases the onus would be on the employer to prove that the original job could not be done on a part-time basis.

If a suitable part-time job at the same level as her original job does not exist the employee might be prepared to take other part-time work at a more junior level and such jobs should be offered to her if they are available. It should not be assumed that she will not be prepared to consider them.

SUBSEQUENT PREGNANCIES

Once an employee has qualified by service for extended maternity leave, she does not have to requalify for subsequent pregnancies. Providing that her total service exceeds the initial qualifying period for the right to return she will be entitled to the same rights for subsequent pregnancies. The legislation does not specify a minimum time between pregnancies.

SMALL COMPANIES

The statutory right to return does not apply to small companies with five or fewer employees (including the woman who is on maternity leave) if it is not reasonably practicable for the employer to allow her to return.

CONTRACTS OF EMPLOYMENT DURING MATERNITY LEAVE

There are two alternative methods of dealing with women on extended maternity leave.

1. The contract of employment may be technically terminated at the end of the 14 week maternity leave period and reactivated with continuous service from the original date of starting when the employee returns;

2. The contract of employment continues but the duty to work is suspended.

In the first case the employee may be treated as a leaver and paid her accrued holiday pay at the end of the 14 week maternity leave period. The P45 is retained until the end of the maternity pay period as statutory maternity pay is subject to deductions for NI and income tax. When she returns, the contract is reactivated with continuous service from the original date of starting.

In the second case the contract remains suspended during the extended maternity leave during which contractual benefits may or may not subsist.

CONTRACTUAL BENEFITS DURING EXTENDED MATERNITY LEAVE

All contractual benefits, except remuneration, must continue to accrue during the 14 week period of basic maternity leave. At the end of the 14 week period it is up to the employer to decide whether contractual benefits continue during the extended period of maternity leave or whether they are suspended.

Employers should establish and publish a policy on contractual benefits during extended maternity leave so that all employees are fully aware of the situation. The following is a list (which is not intended to be exhaustive) of contractual benefits which may be affected:

- accrued holiday entitlement

- company car

- pension fund contributions and benefits

- private health insurance

- permanent health insurance

- life insurance

- subsidised mortgage

The employer also needs to decide whether the extended period of maternity leave counts for contractual benefits based on service, e.g. additional sick pay, holidays, etc. The total period of maternity leave counts for all statutory rights.

The pension fund administrators should be consulted on the options available to employees on extended maternity leave in respect of their pension fund contributions and benefits.

CONTRACTUAL MATERNITY BENEFITS

Some companies provide contractual maternity benefits in excess of those required by law, e.g. full or half pay for part of the maternity leave period or a longer period of maternity leave. In such cases employees may elect to take whichever right is, in any particular respect, the most favourable.

Companies who pay maternity pay in excess of that required by law often make the payment in two parts, a percentage being payable when the employee goes on leave and the balance on her return to work or on completion of a minimum period of service after her return. There is often a proviso requiring her to repay all the contractual maternity pay if she fails to return for the specified period after her maternity leave.

Contractual maternity pay includes SMP to ensure that the employee is not better off as a result of receiving contractual pay plus SMP than she would be if she were working.

HEALTH AND SAFETY

Employers must carry out a risk assessment on any woman who is pregnant, has recently given birth or who is breast feeding. If any health and safety risk is identified then the employer must make any necessary adjustments to the working hours or conditions to eliminate the risk. If this is not possible, then suitable alternative employment must be found if possible. If this is not available then she must be suspended on full pay for the period necessary to protect her health. In particular an employee who is pregnant or has recently given birth may not be required to do night work if she has submitted a medical certificate stating that she should not do this for health and safety reasons.

REDUNDANCY WHILST ON MATERNITY LEAVE

If a woman is made redundant on account of her pregnancy or maternity, the dismissal will be automatically unfair.

If a large scale redundancy arises whilst she is on maternity leave, e.g. a whole establishment, department or section is closed down while one member of staff is on maternity leave, she should be consulted at the same time as everyone else affected by the redundancy. She must be offered suitable alternative employment if it is available. If none is available she will be entitled to redundancy pay based on the total period of her service.

STATUTORY MATERNITY PAY

Statutory Maternity Pay was introduced in 1987 when the responsibility for payment to women on maternity leave passed from the state to the employer, except for those who did not qualify for it on account of length of service.

The Maternity Allowance and Statutory Maternity Pay Regulations 1994 made substantial changes to the system to comply with the Pregnant Workers' Directive from the EC.

To qualify for SMP an employee must:

- have at least 26 weeks' service ending with the 15th week before the EWC (known as the qualifying week).

- earn more than the lower earnings limit (LEL) for NI contributions

- be still pregnant or have given birth by the 11th week before the EWC

- have given her employer 21 days' notice of her intention to take maternity leave

- have stopped working on account of pregnancy

- have provided medical evidence of her expected week of childbirth (form MAT B1)

QUALIFYING WEEK

The qualifying week for SMP is the 15th week before the EWC. In order to qualify for SMP the employee must have at least 26 weeks' service at that date and she must have a valid contract of employment for at least part of that week.

Employees with less than 26 weeks' service at the qualifying week may be able to claim maternity allowance from the DSS provided their contribution record is sufficient for this purpose i.e. if they have paid 26 contributions within 66 weeks ending with the qualifying week.

If a woman is employed at the qualifying week but is not entitled to SMP, the employer should issue her with a form SMP I stating the reason for non-payment. The employee will require this form if she is to claim maternity allowance from the DSS.

NOTIFICATION

In order to qualify for SMP an employee must give her employer at least 21 days' notice of her intention to take maternity leave, if it is reasonably practicable for her to do so. If she fails to give the full 21 days' notice, the employer can withhold SMP if the reason for the late notification is not acceptable. In these circumstances the employee can apply for a formal decision by the adjudication officer. She will be expected to have requested written reasons from her employer for refusal to pay and to have raised the matter through a grievance procedure if one exists.

If the baby is born before the maternity pay period commences, the employee must provide medical evidence of the birth date within 21 days if reasonably practicable. Payment of SMP will commence the week following the birth.

MEDICAL EVIDENCE

Before a woman who is on maternity leave can be paid SMP she must produce evidence of her expected week of childbirth. This is normally the form MAT B1 signed by a medical practitioner or registered midwife and will not be issued earlier than the 14th week before the EWC.

MATERNITY PAY PERIOD

SMP is payable for a total of 18 weeks. The earliest it can commence is the 11th week before the EWC. Employees who are only entitled to the basic 14 weeks maternity leave will therefore forfeit four weeks' SMP.

RATES OF SMP

Employees who satisfy the above conditions are entitled to statutory maternity pay as follows:

- six weeks' pay at 90% normal weekly earnings; followed by
- 12 weeks' pay at the lower rate of SMP

Average weekly earnings are calculated by totalling the employee's gross earnings up to and including the last pay date before the qualifying week and dividing the total by eight. All payments which are subject to deductions for NI and income tax are included e.g. overtime pay, commission, annual bonuses etc. provided they fall within the calculation period.

SMP is paid as a weekly, not a daily, rate. It is forfeited at the lower rate for any week in which the employee works, if only for a few hours, once the maternity pay period has commenced.

SMP should normally be paid weekly or monthly on the employee's usual pay date. Paying it in a lump sum could result in both the employer and employee paying more in NI contributions, and could give rise to difficulties in recovering payment if the employee works or otherwise ceases to be entitled to SMP after the commencement of maternity leave.

NI AND TAX

SMP is subject to deductions for NI and income tax.

WHEN SMP CEASES

SMP ceases:

- when the full entitlement has been paid, or

- when the employee returns to work at the end of the 14 week maternity leave period

- if the employee is taken into legal custody

- if the employee dies

If the employee is taken into legal custody, liability for payment of SMP ceases with the last pay date before she goes into legal custody.

If the employee dies, liability ceases at the week in which the death occurs.

MULTIPLE BIRTHS OR STILLBIRTH

Maternity pay is what its title indicates. It does not increase in the case of a multiple birth.

It is payable in the event of a stillbirth which occurs after the beginning of the 16th week before the EWC.

RECOVERY OF SMP

The employer recovers a percentage of SMP by making deductions from payments made to the Inland Revenue in respect of NI contributions each month. Small employers whose gross NI employers' and employees' contributions do not exceed the limit set by the government can recover the full amount of SMP.

RECORDS

The following records must be kept in respect of SMP:

- dates of notified maternity absence

- the dates of weeks in which SMP was paid and the amount paid in each week

- records of any weeks for which SMP was not paid together with the reason for non-payment

- the MAT BI or other medical evidence provided by the employee related to SMP (photostat copies where the originals are returned to the employee)

PENALTIES

There are a number of penalties ranging from £1,000 to £5,000 for failure to pay SMP, provide information required for the determination of any question arising in connection with SMP, failure to keep the required records or falsifying documents relating to SMP.

ADMINISTRATIVE PROCEDURES

MATERNITY CHECKLISTS

Because of the complexity of the maternity legislation it is useful to have maternity checklists that can be used by whoever in the personnel department is responsible for administering the maternity procedures. This should ensure that no step in the procedure is forgotten or overlooked. They will obviously have to be drawn up to reflect the policies and procedures of the particular organisation but two examples of maternity checklists are shown on pages 129 and 130, one to be used for employees who are only entitled to the 14 weeks basic maternity leave and the other for those entitled to extended maternity leave. These can be adapted as necessary to suit the needs of the organisation.

INFORMATION FOR EMPLOYEES

It is also useful to have information sheets or a booklet to be given to employees when they notify you that they are pregnant.

These should contain:

- information on their statutory rights, i.e.:

  not to be unfairly dismissed

  time off for antenatal care

  maternity leave

  extended maternity leave

  statutory maternity pay

- procedures which they are required to follow re:

  notification of dates of maternity leave

  production of medical evidence

  written confirmation of intention to return
  if required

  written notification of date of return

- company policy on maternity leave and/or pay (if more generous than statutory rights)

- conditions e.g. length of service pertaining to contractual maternity rights

- whether their contract of employment is suspended or technically terminated during maternity leave

- what happens to contractual benefits during extended maternity leave

●whether maternity leave counts towards additional benefits based on long service

●any other policies or procedures relating to maternity leave or pay that the employee should be aware of

An example of information sheets on maternity rights and procedures to be followed by employees who become pregnant is given on the following pages. Information on contractual benefits will have to be drawn up by individual employers to reflect their own policies.

EXAMPLE OF INFORMATION TO BE GIVEN TO EMPLOYEES WHO ARE PREGNANT

MATERNITY RIGHTS AND PROCEDURES

Please read these notes carefully. Failure to follow any of the procedures could result in you losing your statutory maternity rights.

If you are pregnant you have the following rights regardless of your length of service or the number of hours you work.

- Not to be dismissed on account of your pregnancy or maternity

- Time off with pay to attend an antenatal clinic

- 14 weeks' maternity leave

If you have 26 weeks' service at the 15th week before your expected week of childbirth (EWC) you will also be entitled to

- Statutory maternity pay

If you have two years' service or more at the 11th week before the EWC you will be entitled to

- Extended maternity leave

ANTENATAL CARE

If you require time off to attend an antenatal clinic you should advise your immediate manager or supervisor who will require to see your appointment card, except in the case of the first appointment.

cont.

Example of Information (cont.)

14 WEEKS' MATERNITY LEAVE

The 14 weeks' maternity leave can commence at any time from the 11th week before the EWC. In order to qualify for this leave you must give the company at least 21 days' notice in writing of the date you intend to start your maternity leave. You must also tell the company the expected week of childbirth. The company may ask you for a medical certificate signed by your doctor or a qualified midwife confirming the expected week of confinement.

During this leave you will be entitled to all your normal contractual benefits except remuneration. The Personnel Department will explain the contractual benefits covered.

You may continue to work as long as you wish during your pregnancy but if you are absent from work due to a maternity related condition during or any time after the sixth week before the EWC, the company will treat you as having started your maternity leave and will commence payment of statutory maternity pay. If your absence at that time is due to an illness or injury not connected with your pregnancy, your maternity leave will not start until you notify us.

If you wish to return to work before the 14 weeks' leave has expired, you must give the company 7 days' notice of your intention to return early.

cont.

Example of Information (cont.)

EXTENDED MATERNITY LEAVE

If you have 2 years' service or more at the 11th week before the expected week of childbirth, you will be entitled to extended maternity leave. This includes your 14 weeks' maternity leave and you must return not later than 29 weeks from the beginning of the week in which the baby was born. In order to qualify for extended maternity leave you must follow the notification procedure outlined under the 14 weeks' leave heading and in addition indicate your intention to return after the birth of the baby.

Notification of date of childbirth

After the baby is born, you should notify the company in writing of the actual date of childbirth.

Written confirmation of your intention to return

Not less than 21 days before the end of your 14 week maternity leave period the company will write to you and ask if you still intend to return to work. You MUST reply to this letter within 14 days, otherwise you may lose your statutory right to return.

Notifying your date of return

You must give the company at least 21 days' notice in writing of your intended date of return at the end of your extended maternity leave.

cont.

Example of Information (cont.)

Postponement of date of return

If you are taken ill and have to postpone your notified date of return, you must inform the company as soon as possible and send in a doctor's certificate. You must then return within four weeks or on the date specified on the doctor's certificate if this is earlier. You can only postpone your return once. If you are not fit to resume work then you will forfeit your right to return.

The company may ask you to postpone the date of your return for a maximum of 4 weeks. The company will not take this step without good reason which will be given to you at the time.

CONTINUOUS SERVICE

When you return to work following either your 14 week maternity leave period or your extended maternity leave, your service will be continuous from your original date of starting, for all statutory rights.

STATUTORY MATERNITY PAY

If you have 26 weeks' service or more at the 15th week before the expected week of childbirth and earn more than the lower earnings limit for NI contributions, you will be eligible for statutory maternity pay (SMP). This will be paid for a maximum of 18 weeks commencing from the date you start your maternity leave.

cont.

Example of Information (cont.)

In order to qualify for SMP you must comply with the notification requirements outlined above and in addition produce medical evidence, normally on a form MAT B1 signed by your doctor or a registered midwife, of your EWC.

Statutory maternity pay consists of:

- 6 weeks at 90% of your normal average earnings

followed by:

- 12 weeks at (insert current rate)

SMP is paid on your normal pay day and is subject to deductions for NI contributions and income tax. It is a weekly, not an hourly rate, and is forfeited for any week in which you do any work - even a few hours - once you have commenced your maternity leave.

SMP ends

- At the end of the 14 week maternity leave period or,

- After 18 weeks' payment (in the case of employees entitled to extended maternity leave or who do not return after the 14 weeks maternity leave)

cont.

This page may be photocopied without prior permission.
© *The Industrial Society 1994*

Example of Information (cont.)

MATERNITY ALLOWANCE

If you have less than 26 weeks' service you will not be eligible for SMP but you may be able to draw maternity allowance from the Department of Social Security provided you have paid 26 or more NI contributions in the 66 weeks ending with the 15th week before your EWC. The company will give you a form SMP1 which you should take to the DSS when making your claim.

This page may be photocopied without prior permission.
© The Industrial Society 1994

MATERNITY CHECKLIST
(for employees who do not qualify for extended
maternity leave)

Name	
Job Title	
Dept.	
Date of starting	
Date pregnancy notified	
Date information supplied to employee	
EWC	
11th week before EWC	
Date due to commence maternity leave (21 days' notice required)	
Entitlement to SMP YES/NO	
Payroll notified	
MAT B1 seen	
Date due to return	

This page may be photocopied without prior permission.
© *The Industrial Society 1994*

MATERNITY CHECKLIST

(Employees with 2 years' service or more at the
11th week before the EWC)

Name	Dept
Job Title	Date of Starting
Date pregnancy notified	Date information given to employee
EWC	11th week before EWC
Date due to commence maternity leave (21 days' notice required)	
Payroll notified	MAT B1 seen
14 weeks' maternity leave ends:	Actual date of childbirth:
Due to return not later than:	
Written confirmation of intent to return sent (not earlier than 21 days before end of 14 week maternity leave period)	
Intends to return? YES/NO	Notified Date of return
Manager informed	Payroll informed
New contract issued (if appropriate) – service continuous from original date of starting	

This page may be photocopied without prior permission.
© *The Industrial Society 1994*

ABSENCE

A high level of absenteeism is costly to any organisation and the removal of rebate for SSP brought this sharply into focus. It also has a considerable effect on the efficiency of the organisation and results in poor staff morale. It is in itself a symptom of poor morale.

If employees are perceived to get away with a poor attendance record it is extremely discouraging for those who are conscientious. It is therefore in the interests of every organisation to tackle the problem of absenteeism and take positive steps to reduce it.

CONTROLLING ABSENTEEISM – WHOSE RESPONSIBILITY?

It is the responsibility of line management to control absenteeism. Only they are in a position to know who is at work and who is not on any particular day or at any particular time. It is certainly not feasible for the personnel department to undertake this task.

However, the full backing and support of top management is essential for the successful operation of any absence control policy and no attempt to introduce one should be made without their full commitment.

ROLE OF PERSONNEL

Although it cannot be held responsible for the day to day control of absenteeism, the personnel department has a very positive role to play in any formal absence control programme – in fact it may well have instigated it in the first place.

The role of personnel is to:

- Draw up policies and procedures for controlling absenteeism

- Obtain the full commitment of senior management

- Train all managers and supervisors in how to handle problems of absenteeism

- Monitor them to ensure they are effective

- Identify particular problems and bring them to the attention of management

- Ensure that there is a consistent approach throughout the organisation

CALCULATING THE ABSENCE RATE

Before any realistic action can be taken to monitor or control absenteeism the absence rate should be calculated using the following formula.

$$\frac{\text{Number of days lost through absence}}{\text{Average no of employees x number of working days}} \times 100$$

The level of absence should be compared, if possible, with the national average and the average for that particular industry if the figures are available. A survey published by The Industrial Society published in 1993 entitled "Wish you were Here" found the national average was 3.97%. The figure in 1987 when the previous survey was carried out was 5.05%.

There are two other formulae which may be used in connection with the calculation of absence statistics. These are:

The number of employees affected

$$\frac{\text{Number of employees with one or more absence spells in a given period}}{\text{Average number of employees over the same period}} \times 100$$

Average length of absence

$$\frac{\text{Total days lost in period due to absence}}{\text{Number of spells of absence}}$$

ABSENCE RECORDS

The next stage in the absence control procedure is to establish reliable absence records across the whole organisation. These should:

- Show the actual dates of absence for each individual

- Show the reasons for absence in each case

- Show the general level of absence in the department/section/company as a whole

These records must be readily available to all line management in respect of their own staff, preferably by means of computer. If managers are to be required to control the absence levels in their departments, they must be given the tools to do the job. If the records have to be obtained from a number of different sources, e.g. payroll, personnel, etc., busy managers will be deterred from taking the necessary action. It is, of course, essential that the personnel department has easy access to the absence records of all employees.

DEFINING ACCEPTABLE LEVELS OF ABSENCE

In the interests of consistency, a company should issue general guidance on the level at which absence becomes unacceptable. This should be expressed in numbers of days' absence a given period e.g. per month, per quarter, per annum, beyond which action is triggered. It is not recommended to publish these figures to the whole workforce as this might lead to the belief that sick leave below this level is an entitlement which should be taken.

Whilst a consistent approach across the whole organisation is essential, this does not mean that every employee should be treated in exactly the same way. The automatic despatch of a warning letter as soon as the trigger point is reached, regardless of the circumstances, can be very demoralising for an employee with an otherwise excellent attendance record who happens to have had an operation or contracted a serious illness. Each case should be considered on its merits. The personnel department can exercise control by ensuring that no action is taken until the circumstances of each case have been investigated.

PROCEDURES FOR NOTIFYING ABSENCE

Procedures to be followed by employees who are absent due to sickness or other causes need to be spelled out clearly and made known to all employees. Employees should normally be asked to contact their immediate supervisor or line manager by a specific time, if they are unable to come to work for any reason. Wherever possible they should speak to the supervisor or line manager personally. This will enable the manager to establish the facts and ascertain as far as possible how long the employee is likely to be absent. Leaving a message at the switchboard should be strongly discouraged unless there is no alternative.

Special arrangements need to be made for shift or night workers who should be encouraged to notify absence before the shift commences but whose manager or supervisor may not be available to speak to them. It may be necessary in such circumstances for the employee to notify security or the manager or supervisor of the previous shift.

Whilst it is in order to stipulate that employees must notify the company of the reason for their absence by a specific time and payment of contractual sick pay may be dependent on this, statutory sick pay cannot be withheld if the employee has notified the company of the reason for absence at any time on the first day of absence.

SELF-CERTIFICATION

Some managers regard self-certification as "a licence to go sick" and regret that they cannot demand a doctor's certificate until the eighth day of absence. Some still endeavour to control poor attendance in the case of specific individuals by insisting on a doctor's certificate for all absences and are even prepared to pay for the certificate. This defeats one of the main objectives of the introduction of self-certification which was to empty the doctors' surgeries of people requesting pieces of paper to send to their employers to justify their absence. Often the doctor was in no better position to judge whether or not they had really been sick than the employer if what they asked for was a "signing off" certificate. Some medical practices refuse to issue certificates for absences of less than 8 days, even if the patient is prepared to pay for them.

Control of absence is a management problem, not a medical one. Properly used, self-certification is an additional tool which can be used for the benefit of management.

Some organisations do not require self-certificates to be filled in until the employee has been absent for three days or more. To be fully effective, self-certificates should be completed for *all* absences, regardless of their length, and particularly for odd days of absence. They should be filled in as soon as the employee returns to work and the form should contain a warning that any false statement on the part of the employee will lead to disciplinary action.

RETURN TO WORK INTERVIEW

On return to work following absence the employee should be interviewed by the manager or supervisor in order to explore the reason for the absence and discuss any underlying causes. It also signals to the employee that regular attendance is considered important. Employees may think twice before taking the odd day off without good reason if they realise they will have to account for their absence on their return.

FREQUENT SHORT TERM ABSENCE

Frequent short term absence without good cause is disruptive to the business and damaging to morale. It should be dealt with initially by counselling, but if it persists it may be necessary to invoke the disciplinary procedure.

If the short term absences are due to medical reasons employees should be asked to consult a doctor, if they have not already done so, to establish the cause of the problem and whether an improvement could be effected by proper treatment. The employee should be warned of the possible consequences should the frequent absences persist. If the attendance does not improve following further warnings it may become necessary to dismiss the employee, not necessarily because there is any doubt about the genuineness of the illness, but because the absence is adversely affecting the operation of the business.

If the short term absences are due to a temporary personal or domestic crisis, efforts should be made to assist the employee if this is possible. It should be made clear, however, that concessions cannot go on indefinitely and a time limit should be set for the employee to solve the problem. The situation should be reviewed on a regular basis.

If the short term absences are apparently due to a variety of reasons for which no satisfactory explanation can be offered and if informal counselling does not result in an improvement, the disciplinary procedure should be invoked.

All cases of short term absence should be dealt with when they occur. To ignore it is to build up trouble for the future. Some managers are reluctant to tackle the problem but it becomes more difficult to dismiss employees for persistent absence when it has been tolerated over a long period and the employee has two years' service or more.

Special training for managers and supervisors in dealing with problems of absenteeism should be arranged, and this is an important feature of any absence control procedure.

LONG TERM ABSENCE

Long term absence is far less disruptive to the organisation than short term absence. If it is known that an employee is likely to be absent for some considerable time due to an operation or serious illness, contingency plans can be drawn up to cover the job during the absence.

However, if the absence persists for a long time and there is no indication of when the employee will be able to return, it may be necessary to consider whether the employment should be terminated. The reason for dismissal in this case would be capability. Before reaching this decision the employee's length of service and previous record should be taken into account and the following procedures followed.

In all cases of long term absence it is important to:

- Keep in touch with the employee

- Ask when likely to return

- Seek medical advice from the employee's general practitioner if dismissal is contemplated

- Keep employee informed if the job is at risk

- Seek alternative employment if this will solve the problem

- Consider all possible options e.g. part-time work, early retirement, permanent health insurance

- If employment is terminated, pay in lieu of notice.

ACCESS TO MEDICAL REPORTS ACT

When seeking advice from the employee's general practitioner the procedure laid down by the Access to Medical Reports Act 1988 must be followed. The requirements are as follows:

- the employer must notify the employee in writing that a medical report is being sought

- the employee must give consent in writing to the medical report being obtained

- the employee must be informed of his/her rights under the Act which are:

  to withhold consent to the report being sought

  to have access to the report before it is sent to the employer

  to have access to the report after it is sent to the employer

  to request that the report is amended

  to refuse to allow the report to be sent to the employer

The doctor will charge a fee for providing the report. If the employee refuses permission for the employer to consult the medical practitioner, it should be made clear that any decision regarding termination of employment will have to be made on the facts known to the employer without the benefit of medical advice.

In cases of prolonged serious illness it is the employee's general practitioner, not the company doctor, who should be consulted as it is the general practitioner who will be best informed on the state of the employee's health.

Employers are not entitled to ask for confidential medical information. They may only ask

- whether the employee is likely to be able to return to work in the foreseeable future and if so, when

- if the employee is expected to return in the near future, whether he/she will be able to do his/her normal job. A brief description of the job should be enclosed for the doctor's information.

A model letter, approved by the British Medical Association, is included in an appendix to the ACAS handbook "Discipline at Work".

If the doctor advises that alternative work should be sought, the employer should make every effort to comply with the request. In many cases however requests for "light work" cannot be met and in such cases the company is not obliged to create a suitable job.

DISMISSAL

If, following consultation with the employee and the receipt of medical advice it is decided to dismiss the employee, the employee should be paid the statutory or contractual period of notice, whichever is the longer, whether or not he/she is still in receipt of company sick pay. This is a statutory requirement although there is provision in the Employment Rights Act 1996 which takes away this right if the contractual period of notice exceeds the statutory minimum by a period of at least one week.

There is a common belief that an employee cannot be dismissed for long term absence while he/she is still in receipt of company sick pay. This is not necessarily the case. There is nothing to prevent an employer dismissing the employee before the sick pay expires unless there is a contractual term preventing this. However, it would be unreasonable for an employer to dismiss a long service employee with a considerable sick pay entitlement after a comparatively short period of absence. It is particularly important not to dismiss an employee who is on long-term sickness if this would deprive him or her of the right to permanent health insurance. All cases should be considered on their merits.

ABSENCE DUE TO ACCIDENT AT WORK

Some companies are confused as to whether they have the right to dismiss an employee who is absent due to an accident or an alleged accident at work. The two issues should be kept quite separate from each other and the decision as to whether or not to dismiss should be made on the facts of the case following consultation and medical advice. If the employee wishes to make a claim against the company as a result of the accident, this will be a matter for his/her solicitors and the company's insurers. The claim should include compensation for loss of earnings if this is relevant.

PREVENTATIVE MEASURES

RECRUITMENT

When recruiting new employees it is recommended that they should be questioned at interview on their attendance record with their previous employers, particularly the number of days' absence they have had over the past year and the reasons for absence. This is likely to be a good predictor of future behaviour. It may be of course that the employee has had a recent serious illness causing an unusually long period of absence in which case the new employer would need to be satisfied that the person had fully recovered.

When taking up references information on number of days absent over a defined period of not less than one year should be requested. If the reference is unsatisfactory it may be decided not to proceed with the engagement.

PROBATIONARY PERIOD

Absence should be carefully monitored during the probationary period and any necessary action taken early on in the employment relationship if regular attendance appears to be a problem.

OTHER MEASURES FOR DEALING WITH ABSENTEEISM

ATTENDANCE BONUSES

The problem of poor attendance is often tackled with a series of sticks and carrots. One incentive for encouraging good attendance is the introduction of an attendance bonus. This has a number of disadvantages, namely

- Some people consider that regular attendance is an integral part of the job and people should not be paid extra for merely coming to work regularly

- Unless carefully controlled and kept as a separate payment, it can rapidly be absorbed into and seen to be, part of the basic rate for the job

- Bonus payments must be strictly controlled. If the terms of the scheme require the whole bonus to be forfeited for one absence, managers may be tempted to turn a blind eye to the occasional absence for what they consider to be justifiable reasons, leading to possible abuse of the scheme.

It is recommended that if attendance bonuses are introduced they should operate for a short period only and should be discontinued before their effectiveness starts to wear off.

SPECIAL BENEFITS

In some cases additional holiday or special prizes are awarded to employees who have not been absent over the whole year. Where additional holiday is given, the rules need to be carefully worked out.

LEAGUE TABLES

The publication of league tables showing the level of sickness absence by department can generate a spirit of competition resulting in a reduced absence rate.

WITHHOLDING COMPANY SICK PAY

Disincentives such as withholding company sick pay for the first three days of absence are sometimes more effective than the carrots of bonuses or special prizes. Withholding sick pay becomes an option when occupational sick pay is at the discretion of management but where there is a contractual right to sick pay it cannot normally be withdrawn without the consent of the employees.

The introduction of improved or single status sick pay schemes may provide an opportunity to introduce absence control programmes in a way that would prove acceptable to the workforce.

SICK PAY COMMITTEES

Some organisations appoint sick pay committees whose members include both management and employees. These committees consider individual cases of absence and decide whether payment should be made or not. There is normally an appeals procedure built into the system. There is no evidence to suggest that employees are more lenient than managers in deciding who should be paid. They have been known to be stricter as they are in a better position than management to know the real reason for the absence of their colleagues and who is genuinely ill and who is not.

SICK VISITING

Visiting staff absent due to sickness has been introduced by some companies as an aid to absence control. If this procedure is adopted, the visit should be carried out by someone who is not seen to be a threat to the individual e.g. the company nurse, if there is one, or the welfare officer. Such visits should include the long term genuine sickness cases as well as those whose absence is giving cause for concern. Employees who are in hospital appreciate the concern of the company if it is genuine, and those whose reason for absence is suspect are encouraged to return to work.

EXTENDED LEAVE OF ABSENCE

Companies with a large ethnic minority workforce frequently receive requests for extended leave from employees who wish to visit their country of origin.

If many such requests are received an extended leave policy should be drawn up to ensure that everyone is treated fairly. The ACAS handbook "Discipline at Work" recommends that the following should be incorporated in all such policies.

- The policy should apply to all employees regardless of sex, marital status or racial group.

- Any conditions should be explained to the employee before taking leave including penalties for failure to return on time. The employee's signature should be obtained as acknowledgement that the employee understands them.

- if the employee fails to return this should be treated as failure to abide by the rules and investigated appropriately.

- Foreign medical certificates should not be treated in a discriminatory way.

- The employee's age, length of service and previous record should be taken into account together with any explanation, before deciding to dismiss.

When drawing up a policy the following aspects should be considered:

- Minimum period of service required before extended leave is granted

- Maximum period of extended leave permitted at any one time

- How frequently extended leave is permitted e.g. once every three years, five years, etc.

- Whether holiday entitlement is permitted to be carried over from one year to the next for the purposes of taking extended leave

●Whether there are any restrictions as to when extended leave may be taken e.g. not in July or August or at particularly busy times of year

●Penalty for failure to return by the agreed date

The extended leave policy should be published, preferably in the employee handbook, and made known to all employees. Employees who are granted extended leave should be given a letter explaining

●the conditions on which the extended leave is granted

●the date on which they are due to return

●the penalty for failure to return

A signature should be obtained from the employees acknowledging that they fully understand the terms and conditions on which the extended leave of absence is granted. If the employee concerned does not speak English, steps should be taken to ensure that he/she fully understands what the letter contains either by means of an interpreter or, if there are a large number of employees of the same nationality, by having the letter or explanatory leaflet printed in that language.

If the employee fails to return by the appointed date, a full investigation should be instigated to establish the reason for the continued absence. On no account should the employee's service be terminated before a full enquiry has taken place. Automatic termination of employment for failure to return from extended leave of absence could lead to a successful claim for unfair dismissal.

CONTROLLING ABSENTEEISM

CHECKLIST OF GOOD PRACTICE

1. Measure the absence rate – identify problem areas

2. Draw up policies and procedures

3. Obtain commitment of top management

4. Train managers and supervisors who will operate scheme

5. Ensure accessibility of absence records to all line managers and supervisors

6. Establish "trigger points" for taking action

7. Check absence records of new employees before engagement

8. Monitor absence of new starters during probationary period

9. Ensure all staff are aware of absence notification procedures and certification requirements

10. Interview all staff on return to work after sickness absence

11. Initially counsel employees whose absence is unsatisfactory

12. Invoke disciplinary procedure if counselling does not improve the situation

13. Ensure consistency of approach throughout the organisation

REDUNDANCY

Redundancy has been an increasingly familiar phenomenon over the past few years and many employers have had to tackle the situation for the first time.

Redundancy is painful both for the employer and the employee and every effort should be made to mitigate its effects.

In this chapter we will consider three aspects of redundancy

1. The legal aspects

2. Handling the redundancy situation

3. Redundancy counselling

THE LEGAL ASPECTS

DEFINITION OF REDUNDANCY

The legal definition of redundancy is important. It is contained in the Employment Rights Act 1996. This states that redundancy occurs when an employer has ceased, or intends to cease, to carry on the business at which the employee was employed, or has ceased, or intends to cease, to carry on the business at the place where the employee was employed.

Alternatively redundancy will occur when the requirements of a business for employees to carry out work of a particular kind, or for employees to carry out work of a particular kind in that place have ceased or diminished, or are expected to cease or diminish.

From this it can clearly be seen that it is always the job that is redundant, never the person. Some companies see redundancy as an easy option for getting rid of a difficult or unsatisfactory employee but such action can have potentially costly consequences.

UNFAIR DISMISSAL

Redundancy is a "fair" reason for dismissal as defined in the Employment Rights Act 1996 (see Chapter 11). However, claims for unfair dismissal may be brought if:

- the selection for redundancy was unfair

- the method of implementing the redundancy was unfair

The selection for redundancy of a woman who is pregnant or on maternity leave on the grounds of her pregnancy or maternity is automatically unfair.

CONSULTATION WITH EMPLOYEE REPRESENTATIVES

A dismissal on grounds of redundancy may be found to be unfair if proper consultation did not take place before the redundancy was implemented.

The law stipulates that where it is proposed to dismiss 20 or more employees consultation must take place with elected representatives who may be either trade union representatives or elected employee representatives

- as soon as possible and not later than 90 days before the first dismissal if 100 or more employees in one establishment are to be made redundant within a period of 90 days or less

- as soon as possible and not less than 30 days before the first dismissal if 20–99 employees in one establishment are to be made redundant within a period of 30 days or less

●as soon as possible if fewer than 20 employees are to be made redundant

For the purposes of consultation the employer must disclose in writing to the representatives

●the reason for the redundancy

●the numbers and descriptions of employees whom it is proposed to dismiss

●the total number of employees of that description employed at the establishment in question

●the proposed method of selection for redundancy

●the proposed method of implementing the dismissals

●the period over which they will take effect

●the proposed method of calculating any non-statutory redundancy payments

Consultation must be genuine, and must include ways of:

●avoiding the dismissals

●reducing the numbers of employees to be dismissed

●mitigating the consequences of the dismissals

with a view to reaching an agreement.

Whilst minimum timescales are specified for the purpose of consultation, the requirement is to consult "as soon as possible". Once it is clearly established that redundancy will occur, consultation should commence without further delay. Failure to do so at the earliest opportunity could result in a successful claim before an Industrial Tribunal.

If a complaint is made to an industrial tribunal that these provisions have not been complied with, the onus will be on the employer to prove:

(a) that there were special circumstances which made it not reasonably practicable to comply with the requirements; and

(b) that he took all necessary steps to comply with the requirements which were reasonably practicable in the circumstances.

The employer cannot claim as a defence that it was not reasonably practicable to comply with these requirements because a controlling employer (including multi-nationals) did not provide the information within the required timescale.

PROTECTIVE AWARDS

If the industrial tribunal upholds the claim, it may make a "protective award" of one week's pay for each week of the protected period up to a maximum of 90 days' pay in the case of 100 or more redundancies within a 90 day period, and 30 days' pay in the case of 20–99 redundancies over a 30 day period. The amount of the award may vary according to the tribunal's assessment of the seriousness of the employer's default.

Protective awards cannot be offset against pay in lieu of notice or any other payment due under the contract.

NOTIFICATION TO SECRETARY OF STATE

Any employer proposing to make 20 or more employees redundant is required by law to notify the Secretary of State for Employment. The time limits for notification are the same as those applying to consultation with trade unions i.e. 90 days where it is proposed to make 100 or more employees redundant within a 90 day period and 30 days where 20–99 employees are affected within a 30 day period. There is no requirement to notify the Secretary of State if fewer than 20 employees are affected.

Notification is made on form HR1 obtainable from local offices of the Department of Employment.

Failure to notify the Secretary of State in accordance with the laid down provisions may result in a fine of up to £5,000.

Again, failure on the part of a controlling employer to give the necessary notice cannot be used in defence of failure to notify the Secretary of State within the necessary timescale.

CONSULTATION WITH INDIVIDUAL EMPLOYEES

Case law has established that not only elected representatives should be consulted but also the individuals selected for redundancy, whether or not they are members of a recognised trade union, and even if only one individual is affected.

Employees should be offered suitable alternative employment if it is available but if there is no suitable vacancy they should be offered any job that is available, and no assumptions should be made that they will not accept it because it may be of a lower status or carry a lower salary or the hours of work may be significantly different. Consultation should cover as wide an area as possible. For example, the employee may be consulted, if this is an option, on whether he/she wishes to work his/her notice or take payment in lieu. Employees should be involved as much as possible in decisions that affect their lives and no assumptions should be made about their preferences.

TIME OFF TO SEEK ALTERNATIVE EMPLOYMENT

There is a legal requirement to allow employees who are to be made redundant and who qualify for statutory redundancy pay reasonable time off with pay to seek other employment or arrange training. It is good practice to extend this entitlement to all redundant employees regardless of their length of service.

OFFERS OF ALTERNATIVE EMPLOYMENT

Employees who are to be made redundant should, wherever possible, be offered alternative employment either within the same company or an associated one. In the case of a large company the search for suitable alternative employment should extend throughout the group.

Offers of alternative employment must be made before the original contract expires and must contain sufficient information to enable the employee to decide whether or not to accept. Any differences between the existing job and the one that is being offered must be drawn to the attention of the employee. The new offer must take effect within four weeks of the end of the existing contract.

Employees on maternity leave are entitled to the same rights as all other employees in the case of redundancy and must be offered suitable alternative employment, if it is available, in the same way as other employees.

TRIAL PERIODS

An employee who is offered alternative employment which involves a different type of job or different terms and conditions of employment is entitled to a four week trial period. If the new job requires retraining, a longer trial period may be agreed between the parties. If either party terminates the employment during the trial period, the contract is treated as having terminated for the original reason i.e. redundancy with effect from the termination of the previous contract.

The normal notice periods do not apply during the trial period, and this should be made clear to the employee at the time the trial period is agreed. If an extended trial period is agreed this should be in writing, should specify the date on which the trial period ends and state the terms and conditions that will apply if the new appointment is accepted.

If an employee continues to work after the end of the trial period he/she will be deemed to have accepted the new appointment and the right to redundancy pay will be lost.

UNREASONABLE REFUSAL OF SUITABLE ALTERNATIVE EMPLOYMENT

If an employee unreasonably refuses suitable alternative employment, the employer may withhold redundancy pay. If the employee complains to an industrial tribunal, the onus will be on the employer to show that the alternative work was suitable and the employee's refusal unreasonable.

The question often arises when a company relocates its premises to another site whether refusal to accept alternative employment on that site is unreasonable and whether the company is justified in withholding redundancy pay in such circumstances.

Relocation clearly falls under the definition of redundancy (see page 149), so unless employees have a mobility clause in their contracts of employment requiring them to work at other locations or in different areas of the country they would *prima facie* be entitled to a redundancy payment.

Whether the alternative employment offered is "suitable" or not would depend on a number of factors, e.g. distance of the new premises from the existing establishment, availability of transport to get there, whether the employer had taken steps to mitigate any loss on the part of the employee resulting from the relocation, and the personal circumstances of the employee concerned. For example, alternative employment in new premises five miles away might be deemed suitable for a senior manager with a company car but unsuitable for a part-time cleaner who lived across the road from the previous premises, there being no public transport between the two locations. Each case would be judged on its merits in deciding whether the company acted reasonably in withholding redundancy pay.

LEAVING DURING NOTICE

An employee may leave early with the employer's consent during the "obligatory" period of notice without forfeiting the right to redundancy pay. The "obligatory" period of notice is that to which the employee is entitled under the contract of employment. Employees may appeal to an industrial tribunal if they believe the consent has been unreasonably withheld.

An employee who is dismissed for misconduct during the notice period may appeal to an industrial tribunal if the redundancy pay is withheld. The industrial tribunal may grant the redundancy pay in full, in part, or withhold it altogether.

Should an employee die during the notice period, the redundancy payment would be calculated to the date of death.

REDUNDANCY PAY

Employees with not less than two years' service are entitled to the following statutory redundancy payments:

- half a week's pay for each complete year of service that the employee was aged 18–21 inclusive

- one week's pay for each complete year of service that the employee was aged 22–40 inclusive

- one and a half weeks' pay for each complete year of service that the employee was aged 41–64

In the case of employees aged 64–65, statutory redundancy pay reduces by one-twelfth for each complete month that the employee was over 64.

There is a maximum statutory limit on earnings which have to be taken into account when calculating redundancy pay and this figure is normally reviewed by the government each year. There is nothing to prevent employers paying redundancy pay in excess of the statutory minimum, and many companies operate considerably more generous schemes.

Reckonable service for statutory redundancy pay is limited to the last 20 years before redundancy. A ready reckoner is available which shows at a glance the number of weeks' redundancy pay due, taking into account the age and length of service of the employee concerned.

The full cost of redundancy is borne by the employer – there is no government rebate.

Redundancy pay is not subject to tax.

ENTITLEMENT TO NOTICE

In addition to redundancy pay, employees are entitled to their statutory or contractual period of notice (whichever is the longer) or payment in lieu.

WRITTEN STATEMENT OF REDUNDANCY PAYMENTS

Employers are required to give employees entitled to statutory redundancy pay a written statement showing how the statutory redundancy payment is calculated. The penalty for failure to do so is a fine of up to £200. The penalty for failure to supply information following a written request from the employee is a fine of up to £1000.

Employers are also required to give details of the method of calculating any other redundancy pay (in addition to statutory redundancy pay) which the employees will receive.

HANDLING REDUNDANCY

REDUNDANCY POLICY OR AGREEMENT

A number of companies have a policy or agreement on handling redundancies. Such policies or agreements are desirable in that they:

- provide a framework to operate within should redundancy occur

- reduce the risk of unfair practices

A redundancy policy or agreement should preferably be formulated when there is no imminent risk of redundancy occurring so that it can be properly thought through in an objective manner.

A policy or agreement will normally include:

- a general statement of company philosophy on maintaining job security

- measures for minimising redundancy situations

- criteria for selection where redundancy is unavoidable

- consultation procedures to be followed

- method of implementation

- severance terms

- appeals procedure

- measures to be taken to assist employees to find alternative employment

- any provision for redundancy counselling

GENERAL POLICY STATEMENT

This should state the company's commitment to the principle of maintaining job security, minimising the effects of redundancy where it is unavoidable and dealing with it in a fair and consistent manner.

MEASURES FOR MINIMISING REDUNDANCY SITUATIONS

These should be specified and may include:

- restricting recruitment
- reducing overtime
- terminating employees on temporary contracts
- retiring employees over normal retirement age
- retraining employees for other types of work
- redeploying employees surplus to requirements
- temporary lay-off or operating short-time working (if this is provided for in the contract of employment)

CRITERIA FOR SELECTION

The criteria on which selection for redundancy is based is a crucial aspect of redundancy since unfair selection can give rise to a claim for unfair dismissal. The criteria for selection should be agreed with trade union or other employee representatives, should be capable of objective measurement and should be published.

"Last in, first out" (LIFO) is no longer the most common method of selection for redundancy. Whilst it is clearly an objective method of selection, there is a general recognition that it does not always result in retention of those employees best equipped to ensure the future prosperity of the business which may be vital if further redundancies are to be avoided. Skills and flexibility therefore are usually given a much higher priority when criteria for selection are being drawn up.

Examples of options for selection for redundancy include:

- volunteers

- early retirement

- skills and qualifications

- LIFO (last in, first out)

- disciplinary record

- work performance

- attendance record

VOLUNTEERS

Asking for volunteers may considerably ease the situation and reduce the need for compulsory redundancy. A generous compensation package may be offered in order to encourage employees to come forward. However, when asking for volunteers for redundancy the company should make it clear that the management reserve the right to refuse requests for voluntary redundancy if acceptance would result in the company being deprived of the skills and experience it requires to operate the business successfully.

It might be necessary to restrict volunteers to certain departments or categories of staff.

It should also be borne in mind that those most likely to volunteer are those with long service and therefore relatively high compensation packages which will be expensive.

Account should be taken of the effect on morale if the number of volunteers exceeds the required number and some of them are refused redundancy.

EARLY RETIREMENT

Some companies adjust their pension schemes or target their severance payments to encourage employees to take early retirement.

A number of people are happy to do this, bearing in mind the high level of stress in many work situations which older people often feel they can no longer cope with.

SKILLS AND QUALIFICATIONS

As stated above, it is vital for the company to retain those employees with the skills, experience and qualifications that will enable it to survive a lean period and go forward into growth when economic conditions improve. Flexibility and adaptability are also increasingly important in a era of continual change. The retention of staff with the right qualities is therefore a prime consideration. Employers must, however, use objective, measurable criteria when deciding who should be retained on this basis and be prepared to defend their selection, if necessary, at an industrial tribunal.

LAST IN, FIRST OUT

Whilst this may be the most objective method of selection and has been extensively used in the past, especially in unionised organisations, the increased emphasis on skills and adaptability has meant that LIFO now features much lower down the list of criteria than has been customary in the past, frequently coming into operation only when other factors have already been taken into account.

DISCIPLINARY RECORD

It is quite common for employers to stipulate that those who have disciplinary warnings on their record will be the first to go. Provided the warnings have been properly given and recorded in accordance with the company's disciplinary procedure, this should not create a problem.

WORK PERFORMANCE

People whose work performance has been unsatisfactory may also be among the first to be considered for dismissal in a redundancy situation. However, again objective methods must be used to assess work performance. Employees whose unsatisfactory work performance has never been brought to their attention might well have a case for unfair selection for redundancy.

ATTENDANCE RECORD

Poor attendance records are often taken into account when selecting people for redundancy. Again, this should not cause a problem since factual evidence can be produced to justify the selection, but a clear distinction should be made between those employees who have a record of frequent short term absences and those who have had a long spell of absence in an otherwise satisfactory record. A consistent approach across the company is essential.

CONSULTATION PROCEDURES

Consultation procedures have been discussed in detail earlier in this chapter. Agreed consultation procedures in both union and non-union organisations should be spelled out in the redundancy policy or agreement. Provided they are carefully followed this should minimise the risk of being taken to tribunal on the grounds that the method of implementing the redundancy was unfair.

SEVERANCE TERMS

The generosity (or otherwise) of the severance terms will depend largely on the size and resources of the company. They must not, in any case, be less than the minimum statutory redundancy payments. If the company can afford it, a generous redundancy package softens the blow of redundancy, can be of considerable benefit to the individual and is good for the image of the company.

However, some small or medium sized companies may find themselves in difficulties if they start off with generous redundancy payments and then have to make additional staff redundant over a prolonged period when their financial resources are much reduced and they may be struggling for survival.

Severance payments should be agreed in advance with the company's tax inspector before they are published. A severance package, published in advance, might be considered contractual and therefore subject to tax if it had not previously been agreed with the tax inspector.

APPEALS PROCEDURE

A procedure for dealing with appeals against any aspect of the redundancy procedure should be included in the redundancy policy/agreement. It is evidence of good intent on the part of the company and may well take some of the heat and emotion out of the redundancy situation.

ASSISTING EMPLOYEES TO FIND ALTERNATIVE EMPLOYMENT

The policy/agreement may include steps the company is prepared to take in the provision of counselling, time off to attend interviews, use of facilities (telephones, fax machines, word-processors, photocopiers, assistance from secretarial staff etc.) to assist staff who are to be made redundant to find other employment.

GUIDELINES FOR HANDLING A REDUNDANCY SITUATION

Employers faced with a redundancy situation will need to draw up a strategy for handling it. The following are some of the aspects which need to be considered.

Whenever a redundancy situation arises a senior manager, probably the personnel manager, should be appointed to be responsible for drawing up and/or overseeing the procedure.

DATE OF REDUNDANCY

The date when the redundancy is likely to be implemented needs to be established at an early stage, bearing in mind the consultation requirements, the notification to the Secretary of State and the contractual or statutory notice periods of those likely to be selected.

COMPENSATION

If the level of compensation has not already been laid down, it will need to be decided. Some of the factors to be taken into account are as follows:

- Is early retirement to be encouraged?
  If so, what will be the effect on pension rights?

- Is voluntary redundancy to be encouraged?
  If so, how generous can the company afford to be?

- Is pay in lieu of notice to be part of the severance package? If not, will the employees be given the choice of working their notice or taking pay in lieu?

- If it is important that they work their notice, e.g. in a relocation situation, should a loyalty bonus be paid?

- If the company is relocating, what will the relocation package be in terms of (a) removal expenses and (b) increased travelling expenses?

CRITERIA FOR SELECTION

Decide, agree and publish the criteria for selection and method of implementation if not already included in a redundancy procedure agreement.

SET UP APPEALS PROCEDURE

- Decide constitution of appeal panel.

- Specify how appeal is to be made including time limits.

●Establish ground rules for the operation of the panel.

●Determine how decisions are to be communicated.

PLAN COMMUNICATION STRATEGY

●When is consultation to commence?

●What method of communication is to be adopted e.g. mass meetings, small groups of those involved, individual face to face meetings?

●Who is to do the communicating?

●If more than one site is involved, how is communication to be handled to avoid employees hearing about it "on the grapevine"?

●Plan communication with trade union or employee representatives bearing in mind the requirement to communicate "as soon as possible" whilst ensuring that management retain the initiative. In no circumstances should employees be informed of forthcoming redundancies by a shop steward or trade union official.

●Consult genuinely with trade unions, employee representatives and/or individual employees. Consider any suggestions or representations they may make for avoiding or reducing the scale of redundancies or mitigating their consequences and endeavour to reach agreement.

NOTICE OF REDUNDANCY

- At the end of the protected period or following consultation with the trade union, other recognised employee representatives or individuals, give formal notice of redundancy.

- Follow up in writing giving full details of redundancy/severance payments, statutory, contractual or ex gratia, together with details of any other terms or benefits on offer.

EFFECT ON MORALE

A side effect of redundancy is the effect it has on the morale of those who remain. The manner in which the redundancy is handled can have a major impact on the remaining workforce. If it is perceived to have been handled fairly and humanely the long term effects will be less damaging than if it is seen to have been handled in an arbitrary fashion with little or no concern for those involved.

TIMING OF NOTIFICATION

There is no nice way to inform an individual employee that he or she is redundant but some obvious pitfalls can be avoided. The timing of the communication is important. Friday afternoons should be avoided as employees are left to reflect on their fate over the weekend with no one available to answer questions, give advice or provide reassurance. The effect on the employee's family is likely to be worse in these circumstances.

Monday mornings should also be avoided, especially if employees are not permitted to work their notice. People are not usually at their best first thing on a Monday morning and it is not a good time either to convey or receive bad news. Pressures of work are usually higher which may contribute to the redundancy situation being badly handled. Midweek is a better time for the communication to take place. There is time to plan beforehand and managers and supervisors are available to follow up the initial communication with individual meetings, counselling and written confirmation of the details.

INFORMING THE EMPLOYEE

Communicating news of redundancy is never easy, particularly if the individual has long service and is known personally to the manager who has to break the news. The redundancy interview is often badly handled because the interviewer is acutely embarrassed at having to convey the bad news or over–identifies with the recipient who may not in fact react in the manner anticipated.

Managers faced with this unenviable task should endeavour to remain as calm and objective as possible in the circumstances, explain the background and reasons for the redundancy situation and then go on to explain why that particular individual has been selected for redundancy. Obviously the situation is easier to explain if a whole section or department is closing down and everyone in that section is being made redundant. It is much more difficult if only a few people are involved or the reason for the selection reflects adversely on the employee.

It is important to give the person involved time to absorb the full implication of the news. Managers should resist the temptation to preclude any adverse reaction on the part of the employee by putting up barriers such as talking non-stop. A certain amount of silence may be desirable to enable the employee to digest what has been said and formulate any questions.

Do not procrastinate. Some managers, when faced with the prospect of conveying bad news will talk of almost anything else at the interview in order to avoid coming to the point. This only makes the situation harder for both the employer and the employee. Come to the point quickly and keep the communication as factual as possible.

Do not, on the other hand, rush through the facts at great speed in your anxiety to get the whole episode over and done with as soon as possible. Watch carefully to see that the employee is taking in what you say – he or she may be shell-shocked, especially if the news was unexpected. Watch the body language and respond accordingly.

Be sympathetic, but not over-sympathetic. It is not helpful to the employee to be encouraged to wallow in despair.

Be prepared for the employee to react emotionally – bursting into tears or reacting very angrily to the news. Try to understand the reaction without being carried along by it. Allow the employee to express the emotion before trying sympathetically to calm the situation. It is advisable not to prolong the interview in these circumstances but to reconvene the meeting later when the employee may be more capable of absorbing the details.

Sometimes employees appear to be unable to take in the news due to shock. This can occur even when the redundancy is not totally unexpected, especially if the person has been with the organisation a long time. Again if this is the reaction it is better to terminate the interview and reconvene later in the day when the employee has had time to take in the full implication of the news.

FOLLOW-UP PROCEDURES

The administrative procedures need to be set up in advance. The redundancy pay and notice entitlement must be researched in advance for each employee and the letter setting out the full details should be sent to each employee as soon as formal notice has been given. It is important that they are given this information as soon as possible so that they know what their financial situation is going to be and are able to plan. They will also need to know their options under the company pension scheme if there is one and they are members of it.

If redundancy counselling is not offered, managers should make themselves available for follow-up interviews to answer questions arising from the redundancy situation and resolve any problems resulting from it.

REDUNDANCY COUNSELLING

If the company decides to offer redundancy counselling to its employees there are three basic options to consider:

- to use an outplacement agency
- to bring in external consultants
- to use in-company resources

In addition to helping the employee come to terms with the redundancy situation, redundancy counselling usually includes some or all of the following:

- Tests or counselling designed to identify what type of work the redundant employee might be suitable for. Redundant employees are encouraged to consider other types of employment or a career change if there is not a significant requirement for the type of work they have been engaged in.

●Advice on how to write CV's or letters of application and the best way to approach companies of interest to them.

●Advice or practical sessions on how to be interviewed.

●Advice on "networking" - establishing contacts with ex-colleagues, acquaintances, contacts from previous jobs or anyone who may be able to assist in finding employment.

●Advice on how or where to obtain information about various companies or organisations.

●Advice on how to set up one's own business, if appropriate.

●Advice on how to make "getting a job their job".

OUTPLACEMENT ORGANISATIONS

Outplacement organisations provide a very comprehensive service with all the necessary skills and equipment. Redundant employees may use their premises as a base and have the use of typing services, photocopiers, telephones, fax machines etc. Redundancy programmes vary in length, but the use of premises and regular contact with their advisers and other people who have been made redundant provide useful support. The fact that they have an office to go to is in itself an advantage. The disappearance of structure to their lives and the deprivation of the social contacts which are part of the normal work situation are two of the major problems to be overcome in a redundancy situation.

Outplacement agencies are, however, expensive and their services are usually reserved for redundant senior executives for whom companies are prepared to pay a considerable fee to receive their services.

REDUNDANCY CONSULTANTS

Redundancy consultants usually operate on the employer's premises and the employer agrees in advance the length and content of the programme and the fee to be paid.

IN-HOUSE

This is the least expensive option but it is essential to choose those who are to carry out the counselling with care and ensure that they have the necessary skills. Special training may be required to equip them for the task. The disadvantage of using in-house staff to do the counselling is that they may be associated with the management who made the employees redundant and consequently the level of resentment against them may be greater than would be the case if outside consultants were used.

REACTIONS TO REDUNDANCY

As discussed above, people who are made redundant may experience a number of emotions including shock, anger, disbelief, bitterness, resentment, rejection, helplessness, euphoria or apathy. One of the principal roles of the counsellor is to help them to come to terms with these feelings and respond positively to the situation they find themselves in. Redundancy has been likened to bereavement and can have a very devastating effect on the individual, especially if be or she has worked for the company for a long time. If the redundancy is unexpected, the shock can be overwhelming but even if the redundancy is expected people can still react with disbelief when it happens to them. Every effort should therefore be made by the employer to mitigate the problem.

The biggest problem is likely to be that of overcoming the loss of confidence and self-esteem which results from losing one's job. If the counsellor is able to assist in rebuilding this lost confidence, this will be a major achievement in itself.

WHAT THE EMPLOYER CAN DO

If external consultants are used or counselling takes place in-house, the employer can greatly assist the situation by ensuring that typing services and the use of telephones, photocopiers, stationery etc. are made available to redundant employees during the notice period.

Where large numbers of redundancies are involved, "Job shops" may be set up at which all internal vacancies and any external vacancies known to the employer are advertised. Contact should be made with as many local employers as possible to ensure that the company is advised of any vacancies which might be suitable for the redundant employees. Close contact should also be maintained with the local Job Centre, especially where manual workers are being made redundant.

Employees should be given as much time off, within reasonable limits as they require to attend interviews or arrange training, regardless of their length of service. If they are being made redundant for reasons other than relocation of the establishment they work at they probably have insufficient work to do anyway and the company has little to lose.

Redundancy can happen to anyone at any time.
Good practice requires that employers act reasonably and
with compassion in their handling of redundancy situations.

Handling a redundancy situation well usually passes
largely unnoticed by the press and the general public.
Handling a redundancy situation badly can do untold
damage to the company's reputation and the morale of
those who remain.

DISCIPLINE

The Employment Rights Act 1996 requires all organisations who employ 20 or more employees to provide certain information regarding disciplinary procedures namely:

- a note specifying any disciplinary rules affecting the employee

- a person to whom the employee can apply if dissatisfied with any disciplinary decision

Most disciplinary rules and appeals procedures are incorporated into a disciplinary procedure.

DRAWING UP A DISCIPLINARY PROCEDURE

Disciplinary procedures must comply with the ACAS Code of Practice on Disciplinary Practice and Procedures in Employment. If you are required to draw up a disciplinary procedure, the ACAS advisory handbook "Discipline at Work" is available from all ACAS offices and is an essential reference book for this purpose.

ESSENTIAL FEATURES OF A DISCIPLINARY PROCEDURE

The ACAS Code of Practice sets out the following essential features of disciplinary procedures.
They should:

- be in writing
- specify to whom they apply

- provide for matters to be dealt with quickly

- indicate the disciplinary actions which may be taken

- specify the levels of management which have the authority to take the various forms of disciplinary action, ensuring that immediate superiors do not normally have the power to dismiss without reference to senior management

- provide for individuals to be informed of the complaints against them and to be given an opportunity to state their case before decisions are reached

- give individuals the right to be accompanied by a trade union representative or by a fellow employee of their choice

- ensure that, except for gross misconduct, no employees are dismissed for a first breach of discipline

- ensure that disciplinary action is not taken until the case has been carefully investigated

- ensure that individuals are given an explanation for any penalty imposed

- provide a right of appeal and specify the procedure to be followed

When drawing up a disciplinary procedure, the following aspects must be considered.

WARNINGS

- how many warnings are to be included in the procedure

- who has the authority to give them

- how long are they to remain on record and are they to be removed from the record on expiry or treated as "spent"

Whilst employers may stipulate how many warnings their disciplinary procedure should have, most disciplinary procedures contain three warnings. These are:

- formal verbal warning

- first written warning

- final written warning

It is usually preferable for warnings to be given by the immediate line manager who is in possession of all the facts of the case. It also ensures that senior managers are free to hear appeals as they have not been involved in the warning procedure. However, it is advisable that all written warnings should be vetted or "ghost-written" by the personnel department in case they are required as evidence at a future industrial tribunal hearing.

All written warnings should state:

- the reason for the warning

- the standard required

- the time limit for achieving the required standard

- the penalty for failure to achieve it

- the right of appeal

The procedure should state that subsequent warnings need not necessarily be for the same reason as the first warning and any misconduct or poor performance following a warning will result in a further penalty.

Provision should be made for the procedure to be entered at a later stage in cases of serious misconduct. Some cases may be serious enough to warrant a "first and final" warning.

It should be decided how long warnings should remain on record or treated as active. The most usual periods are six months for verbal and 12 months for written warnings but other periods may be specified to suit the organisation. There are two ways of treating warnings which have expired. They can either be removed from the record entirely or left on the record and treated as "spent". The disciplinary procedure should state which alternative will apply. If the first option is adopted, a system must be put into place to ensure that warnings are removed at the due date.

WITNESSES OR REPRESENTATIVES

The ACAS Code of Practice states that all employees must be given the right to be accompanied by a trade union representative or by a fellow employee of their choice. Some organisations widen this to allow the employee to be accompanied by a friend or relative not connected with the organisation and this can be quite effective.

Being accompanied by a friend of relative may be more comfortable for the employee who may feel inhibited or embarrassed at asking a fellow employee to accompany him or her to a disciplinary hearing unless the fellow employee is already a good friend or known to be sympathetic to the employee's cause. Other employees may, in turn, be reluctant to accompany them in case they become tainted if disciplinary action is meted out to their colleague. Managers who are being disciplined may find it particularly difficult to find a suitable "fellow employee" to accompany them if they work in a small office where there is no one else at their level. Most employers draw the line at allowing a legal representative to attend a disciplinary hearing, certainly at the warning stages. If the disciplinary procedure does not make provision for a legal representative to be present, management are within their rights to refuse to allow one to attend.

INITIAL COUNSELLING

Except in cases of serious misconduct, any shortcomings in employees' conduct or performance should be brought to their attention informally by their immediate manager or supervisor before the formal disciplinary procedure is invoked. Sometimes all that is needed is a counselling interview. If counselling does not result in the required improvement, then the formal disciplinary procedure will come into operation.

Managers and supervisors should beware of allowing a counselling interview to turn inadvertently into a disciplinary interview. If during the course of the interview it becomes apparent that discipline is necessary, the meeting should be terminated and a separate disciplinary hearing convened at a future date.

DISCIPLINARY HEARINGS

All disciplinary action MUST be preceded by a disciplinary hearing.

When asked to attend a disciplinary hearing, employees should be informed of the complaint against them and of their right to be accompanied by a witness or representative. They should be given sufficient notice of the hearing to enable them to find a suitable witness and prepare their case.

It is advisable for the manager conducting the disciplinary hearing to have a witness present to take notes of the meeting. This is particularly important if the employee is accompanied.

At a disciplinary hearing the manager should introduce those present, explaining if necessary why they are there, and then:

- state the case against the employee giving all necessary details

- ask the employee to state his/her case and give an explanation for the misconduct/poor performance

- call witnesses if necessary, e.g. if the evidence is disputed

- adjourn the hearing to consider the facts and decide what penalty, if any, is appropriate

- resume the hearing to inform the employee of the outcome

- advise the employee of the right of appeal

- record the disciplinary action

- in the case of a written warning, follow up in writing to the employee

- monitor and follow up

The monitoring and follow-up are particularly important. If a date for achieving the required standards is set, this should be noted in the diary and follow-up interview to review performance arranged. However, it is not necessary to await the review date if further misconduct or unacceptable performance on the part of the employee occurs before this date. Disciplinary action should always be taken at the time of the misdemeanour. Postponement may be interpreted by the employee as condonation.

If the employee is being disciplined for poor timekeeping or absenteeism it is better to set a long period for monitoring and review. The employee may manage to come in on time for four weeks and then regress into bad habits once the threat of further disciplinary action is removed. Keeping it up for several months is a much better test of the employee's resolve.

DISMISSAL

Dismissal is the final stage of the disciplinary procedure. It should be preceded by a disciplinary hearing following the procedure outlined above. Except in cases of gross misconduct, the employee is entitled to the notice period specified in the contract of employment. It is usual practice to pay in lieu of notice in such cases as the continued presence of an employee who has been dismissed can be damaging both to the company's business and the morale of other employees.

OTHER SANCTIONS

Some disciplinary procedures provide for sanctions other than warnings or dismissal, e.g. demotion, transfer or suspension without pay. If such sanctions are included in the procedure it should be made clear that these form part of the contract of employment.

If they are not included in the procedure, it may be possible to substitute one of these sanctions for dismissal by agreement with the employee who might be prepared to accept demotion or suspension without pay if the penalty were otherwise dismissal. However, it is important to bear in mind that any variation from the standard disciplinary procedure might be regarded as a precedent. It should only be adopted where there are mitigating circumstances which could be defended at a tribunal.

GROSS MISCONDUCT

Some offences committed by employees may be so serious that they are regarded as gross misconduct, the penalty for which is summary dismissal i.e. dismissal without notice or payment in lieu. Disciplinary procedures should give examples of the types of offences which constitute gross misconduct although it is important to state that the list is not to be regarded as exhaustive.

Examples of gross misconduct are:

- assault

- theft from the company or fellow employee

- fraud or falsification of company records, expense claims etc.

- being in possession of or under the influence of illegal drugs

- being under the influence of alcohol to the extent that work performance is seriously impaired

- gross negligence

- malicious damage to company property

- insubordination or refusal to carry out a reasonable instruction

- abuse

- any criminal offence affecting employment

- flagrant disregard of company health and safety regulations

Employees who are dismissed for gross misconduct should not be paid money in lieu of notice. Payment in such circumstances could seriously undermine the company's case at an industrial tribunal.

SUSPENSION

Employees who have committed gross misconduct should be suspended on full pay while a full investigation is carried out. The suspension should be for as short a period as possible to enable the facts to be gathered. The employee should then be asked to attend a disciplinary hearing.

Employees may not be suspended without pay unless provision for this is made in the contract of employment.

TRADE UNION OFFICIALS

Normally, disciplinary action in the case of a shop steward or other trade union representative, except for an oral warning, should not take place until the matter has been discussed fully with a senior trade union representative or full time official. Where there is a recognised trade union, the procedure for disciplining shop stewards should be specified.

SHIFT AND NIGHT WORKERS

Provision should be made for dealing with disciplinary matters in the case of shift or night workers or workers in remote locations where management with the necessary authority to hold disciplinary hearings may not be present. Normally the employee should be suspended on full pay until management can investigate the situation and take the necessary action.

CRIMINAL OFFENCES

Disciplinary action should not be taken automatically against an employee who is charged with, in custody for, or convicted of, a criminal offence. The question to be decided is whether the criminal offence has any bearing on the employment. If the implications of the offence render the employee unsuitable to continue in his/her job, then a disciplinary hearing should be convened. If the employee is unable to attend because he/she is in custody, the employee should be invited to make representations in writing or send a representative to the hearing. The ACAS handbook recommends that the employee should be advised in writing that unless further information is provided a disciplinary decision will be taken on the basis of the information available and could result in dismissal.

It is not necessary to wait for the outcome of a court case to decide whether to dismiss or not. Case law has established that if you have a genuine belief based on reasonable grounds following a thorough investigation that the person committed the offence concerned, it may be fair to dismiss that person without waiting for the outcome of the case.

If the custodial sentence is a long one or if it is likely to be a long time before the case comes before the courts, it may be necessary to dismiss the employee on the grounds that he/she is not available for work and it is not possible to keep the job open for the period of time that would be necessary. In such circtimstances, in order to determine whether or not the dismissal is reasonable, the employer should take into account the employee's length of service and previous record and the period of time that such an employee would normally be permitted to be absent due to sickness before dismissal proceedings are contemplated.

APPEALS

The appeals procedure must be clearly defined and employees should be informed at the disciplinary hearing of the procedure to be followed if they wish to appeal and this should be confirmed it in the follow-up letter.

It is advisable to stipulate that appeals should be in writing and should be made within a stipulated time, e.g. seven or 14 days, from the date of the disciplinary action.

Except in the case of very small companies, the person who took the disciplinary action should not be involved in the appeal. The appeal should be heard by the next level of management above or a senior manager who has not been involved in the disciplinary procedure. The manager hearing the appeal should examine the reason for the appeal and pay particular attention to any new evidence. The manager may adjourn the meeting to consider the decision. The manager should inform the employee of the result of the appeal and the reasons for the decision. The outcome of the appeal should be confirmed in writing.

If the employee is appealing on technical grounds, e.g. that the correct disciplinary procedure had not been followed, the manager hearing the appeal may decide that the original disciplinary hearing should be disregarded and a new one held in its place to ensure that the proper procedures are followed. Failure to follow a laid down procedure is likely to result in a successful claim for unfair dismissal, however justifiable the reason for dismissal.

WRITTEN REASONS FOR DISMISSAL

Any employee with two years service or more has a legal right to request written reasons for dismissal. The employer is required to provide this information within 14 days of the request being made unless this is not reasonably practicable. As this letter may form the basis for a claim for unfair dismissal, it should be composed with care.

Women who are dismissed while they are pregnant or on maternity leave have an automatic right to written reasons for dismissal whether they ask for them or not.

ROLE OF PERSONNEL

Generally speaking members of the personnel department should not get directly involved in disciplinary proceedings i.e. disciplinary hearings or appeals, although they may sometimes attend disciplinary hearings to give support to or act as witness for the manager. If they do this they cannot, of course, get involved in the appeals procedure.

The principal role of the personnel department is to

- draw up the disciplinary procedure if there is not one in existence

- monitor disciplinary action so that a consistent approach is adopted throughout the organisation

- vet or "ghost-write" warning letters and letters of dismissal

- ensure that disciplinary action is taken when necessary

- provide support to line management on disciplinary matters

- ensure that line management are properly trained to handle disciplinary matters

- prepare the industrial tribunal case!

MONITORING DISCIPLINARY ACTION

Monitoring the disciplinary action to ensure a consistent approach is an important aspect of the personnel officer's job. No one else, apart from very senior management, who usually have more pressing matters on their minds, has the same overall view.

Different managers frequently apply different standards in similar situations. Action which results in a verbal warning in one department can provoke a "first and final" in another unless the situation is being monitored. Serious problems can arise if evidence is produced at an unfair dismissal case before an industrial tribunal that a similar situation was treated more leniently in another part of the organisation and did not result in dismissal.

The personnel officer or manager would be wise to insist that all disciplinary matters are discussed with him/her before any disciplinary action is taken by line managers.

Problems arise in cases of misconduct where managers have failed to apply the disciplinary procedure at the right time and then have over-reacted when they could no longer tolerate the employee's conduct and short-circuited the disciplinary procedure.

Many managers are reluctant to take disciplinary action. They may dislike or fear conflict or confrontation and hope that if they do nothing, the problem will go away. This is a recipe for disaster. In such circumstances the personnel department can provide valuable support by advising the manager on the action to be taken and attending the disciplinary hearing in a witness/support role.

It is essential that the personnel department identifies potential disciplinary situations before the situation gets out of hand so that the disciplinary procedure is invoked in good time.

NEW EMPLOYEES

A system should be established for monitoring the progress of all new employees, whether there is a formal probationary period or not, so that any problems can be identified and dealt with at the time they arise and certainly well before the employee has acquired two years' service and the right to claim unfair dismissal.

MANAGEMENT TRAINING

The importance of training managers in disciplinary procedures cannot be stressed too strongly. Such training is better done in-house, either using an outside training organisation or consultant, who should be fully briefed on the company's disciplinary procedure, or by the company's personnel department.

Such training should include familiarisation with the company's disciplinary procedure, the number of warnings, penalties which may be imposed, rights of appeal etc. It should also include role plays on how to conduct a disciplinary hearing, the procedure to be followed, when to adjourn the hearing, penalties to be imposed and the importance of follow-up. Attendance at an industrial tribunal hearing can be a salutary experience and a great deterrent to short-circuiting the system!

A disciplinary checklist is shown on page 192.

DISCIPLINARY CHECKLIST

GET THE FACTS

Timekeeping/absence

- ●Obtain records of

  dates of absence/lateness

  reasons for absence/lateness

  compare records with average for rest of department

Poor performance

- ●be able to quote/show examples of poor performance
- ●check whether training/adequate supervision has been given

Misconduct

- ●interview witnesses
- ●obtain statements
- ●be prepared to call witnesses if necessary

Gross misconduct

- ●suspend on full pay
- ●interview witnesses
- ●obtain written statements
- ●be prepared to call witness if necessary

cont.

Disciplinary Checklist (cont)

Fraud-falsification of documents etc.

- suspend on full pay

- carry out full investigation

- make sure you have sufficient evidence to justify accusation

Decide whether disciplinary action is necessary or appropriate. If so, arrange a disciplinary hearing.

ARRANGING DISCIPLINARY HEARING

Request employee to attend disciplinary hearing, informing him/her of:

- the reason for the hearing

- the right to have a witness or representative present

Ensure that employee has sufficient time to:

- find a suitable witness

- prepare his/her case

Arrange for management witness to attend the hearing and take notes.

cont.

Disciplinary Checklist (cont)

DISCIPLINARY HEARING

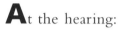

At the hearing:

- introduce those present

- state the complaint against the employee, including the evidence that has been gathered

- invite the employee to state his/her case

- consider any explanation put forward and question further if necessary

- adjourn the hearing to investigate new facts if they emerge

- with the agreement of the employee, call witnesses to support allegations or if evidence is in dispute

- decide if penalty should be applied, adjourning the hearing to make the decision except in very straightforward cases.

When deciding penalty take into account:

- the employee's length of service and previous record

- the type of penalty that has been imposed in similar circumstances in the past

- any mitigating circumstances

Reconvene the meeting to inform employee:

- penalty to be imposed

- reason for penalty

- standard required   *cont.*

Disciplinary Checklist (cont)

●time limit for achieving the required standard

●further penalty for failure to achieve required standard

●right of appeal

FOLLOW UP

If verbal warning, make a diary note or a note in the individual's file of the date warning was given, the reason for the warning and the review period.

If written warning, confirm all details in writing.

Arrange formal review meeting or monitoring process.

Keep records securely, ensuring that confidentiality is maintained.

DISMISSAL

Conduct hearing as above.

Decide whether to allow employee to work notice or whether to pay in lieu. DO NOT pay in lieu of notice in cases of gross misconduct.

SHOP STEWARDS

Do not proceed beyond a verbal warning without informing the district official of the trade union.

DISMISSAL

Avoiding claims of unfair dismissal is one of the major preoccupations of most personnel departments. It is impossible to avoid the risk completely, however carefully one follows the correct procedures. There is always the awkward employee who will go to tribunal, whether he or she has a reasonable case or not. Others may accept dismissal calmly without any intention of taking the matter further until their friends and relatives convince them that they should exercise their rights.

Whilst it is not possible to avoid industrial tribunals altogether, the risk of losing a case can be minimised by:

- having well established disciplinary procedures and following them

- ensuring that line managers consult the personnel department BEFORE taking disciplinary action and certainly before dismissing any employee

- training line managers in all aspects of unfair dismissal

QUALIFYING SERVICE

In order to qualify for the right to claim unfair dismissal the employee must have two years' service with the company. No qualifying service period is required for claims of unfair dismissal arising from sex, race or disability discrimination, trade union activities or pregnancy/maternity.

CONSTRUCTIVE DISMISSAL

An employee's resignation which is justified because of the employer's conduct is treated as a dismissal, i.e. a constructive dismissal, and the employee can complain of unfair dismissal. The test is whether there has been a fundamental breach of contract e.g. a unilateral change in working hours, a reduction in pay or transfer to different work. Constructive dismissal can also be claimed if the employer has breached an implied term of the contract such as mutual trust and confidence by swearing at an employee, for example or severely reprimanding a manager or supervisor in the presence of his or her subordinates.

FAIR DISMISSAL

There are five fair reasons for dismissal. These are:

- conduct

- capability

- redundancy

- contravention of a statutory requirement

- some other substantial reason sufficient to justify dismissal

In a claim for unfair dismissal it is for the employer to establish the reason for dismissal and the tribunal must then decide whether the employer acted reasonably or unreasonably in treating that reason as sufficient for dismissal. Among the factors taken into account are the size and administrative resources of the company and whether the company followed the guidelines laid down in the ACAS Code of Practice on Disciplinary Practice and Procedures.

CONDUCT

Dismissals on the grounds of conduct are fairly common but in all cases it is essential that the company's disciplinary procedure is scrupulously followed. Failure to do so will almost certainly result in the dismissal being found to be unfair, no matter how justified the employer was in taking the action.

GROSS MISCONDUCT

Dismissals for gross misconduct must *always* be preceded by a disciplinary hearing (see previous chapter) no matter how heinous the offence. In many cases the employee will have been suspended on full pay between the time the gross misconduct was committed and the disciplinary hearing.

If, following the disciplinary hearing, the decision is taken to dismiss the employee for gross misconduct, on no account should the employee be paid in lieu of notice as this would seriously weaken the employer's case at an industrial tribunal.

CAPABILITY

Dismissal on the grounds of capability can be of two kinds:

1. Capability related to work performance
2. Capability related to health

SUB–STANDARD WORK

The ACAS handbook "Discipline at Work" sets out the procedure that should be followed where the employee fails to meet a satisfactory level of performance. In broad terms these are:

- employees must be made aware of the standards of performance that are expected of them

- employees who fall short of this standard should be interviewed and an explanation sought

- additional training should be offered wherever practical to assist the employee to reach the required standard

- consideration should be given to the possibility of offering alternative work

- employees should be warned of the consequences of continued failure to meet the required standard

- if the unsatisfactory performance still continues, the employee should be dismissed with notice or payment in lieu

ACTION IN SERIOUS CASES

The ACAS handbook points out that where the employee commits a single error which has actual or potential consequences that are extremely serious for the company, warnings will not normally be appropriate. It suggests that the disciplinary procedure should make it clear that dismissal will take place in such circumstances.

LONG SERVICE EMPLOYEES

Long service employees whose sub-standard performance has been tolerated over a number of years can cause a problem if there is a change of management. To dismiss the employee on the grounds of capability, even after warnings had been given, would be risky. An industrial tribunal would want to know why action to remedy the situation had not been taken many years earlier. The argument that previous management had been remiss or incompetent in this matter is not acceptable. The company is responsible for the acts and omissions of its managers and therefore the company, not the individual manager, would be deemed to be responsible for the failure to act.

In such circumstances the company should consider options other than dismissal such as early retirement, transfer to more suitable work, or termination by mutual agreement following a negotiated settlement or compromise agreement.

CAPABILITY ON GROUNDS OF ILL-HEALTH

The method of dealing with long term sickness absence is dealt with at length in the chapter on Absence. The main risks of a claim for unfair dismissal are dismissing a long-service employee after a relatively short period of absence, failing to carry out a proper investigation of the reasons for absence and failing to seek medical advice before deciding to dismiss.

REDUNDANCY

Redundancy is a fair reason for dismissal but there are two aspects of handling redundancy which could give rise to a claim of unfair dismissal. These are:

- Unfair selection for redundancy
- The method of implementing the redundancy was unfair

These two aspects, the importance of establishing objective criteria for selection for redundancy and methods of handling the redundancy situation, are fully discussed in chapter 9.

CONTRAVENTION OF A STATUTORY REQUIREMENT

It is fair to dismiss someone if, by continuing to employ them, the company would be breaking the law. One obvious example is continuing to employ a driver who has lost his/her licence. However, in such cases a company would be expected to seek suitable alternative employment within the organisation if practicable before dismissing the individual. Again it is not sufficient to rely on the "fair" reason for dismissal – the employer must also act reasonably in treating it as a fair reason.

Dismissal of an illegal immigrant or someone not entitled to work in the UK would fall under this heading.

SOME OTHER SUBSTANTIAL REASON

This covers all other contingencies which do not fall within the scope of the other fair reasons. The most frequent reason for dismissal under this heading is business need, e.g. a reorganisation involving a change in hours of work with which the employee cannot or will not comply. Once again the tribunal must decide whether the employer acted reasonably in treating it as sufficient to justify dismissal. In order to have a chance of succeeding, such reorganisations would have had to result from genuine business need and not administrative convenience.

TRADE UNION ACTIVITIES

It is automatically unfair to dismiss an employee on the grounds that he/she

(a) was, or proposed to become, a member of an independent trade union;

(b) had taken, or proposed to take, part at any appropriate time in the activities of an independent trade union; or

(c) had refused, or proposed to refuse, to become or remain a member of a trade union which was not an independent trade union.

PREGNANCY

It is automatically unfair to dismiss a woman because she is pregnant or on maternity leave.

THE ORIGINATING APPLICATION

An employee who wishes to claim unfair dismissal fills in an "originating application" on a form IT1 which can be obtained from any Job Centre. The employee is required to give an account of the events leading up to the dismissal and also provide certain employment details. He/she is also asked to state whether, in the event of a successful conclusion to the tribunal hearing, reinstatement is required or compensation. The completed form is sent to the Office of Industrial Tribunals who then forward it with a form IT3 to the employer.

The employer has 21 days to fill in the IT3, and return it to the Office of Industrial Tribunals. The employer is required to state the reason for the dismissal and give their account of the events leading up to the dismissal. The employer must also confirm the employment details (dates of starting, leaving, rate of pay etc.) submitted by the employee.

This form should be completed with great care because the information on it forms the basis of the case. In particular, if there were a number of reasons for the employee's dismissal, it is important to decide which is the principal reason. Cases have been lost because employers have chosen the wrong grounds on which to resist it. Had they argued the case on different grounds, they might have succeeded.

CONCILIATION BY ACAS

When the IT3 reaches the Office of Industrial Tribunals, ACAS will contact both parties and try to effect a conciliation i.e. a settlement out of court.

The employer may decide to settle at this point, particularly if there are doubts as to whether the company will win the case. The company may decide that it does not in any case wish to proceed with the case bearing in mind the costly and time-consuming effort required to prepare it.

If, on the other hand, the employer believes he has a strong case or objects strongly on principle to paying money to someone who has perhaps committed gross misconduct, then the case will proceed to Tribunal.

TRIBUNAL PROCEDURE

An Industrial Tribunal consists of one employer's representative, one trade union representative and a legally qualified chairman.

Each side presents its case to the tribunal and may call witnesses. Each side will cross-examine the other and sum up its own case at the end of the hearing. The tribunal will then retire or ask the parties to retire while it considers its decision. This is usually communicated to the parties on the same day with a brief resume' of the reasons why the tribunal reached that decision. Tribunal decisions are conveyed to the parties in writing at a later date. If the tribunal has difficulty in reaching a decision, the tribunal may be adjourned and the decision communicated later. Tribunal decisions do not have to be unanimous.

APPEALS

Appeals against tribunal decisions can only be made on a point of law and must be made to the Employment Appeals Tribunal within 42 days of the receipt of the written decision. Further appeals can be made to the Court of Appeal and the House of Lords.

REMEDIES

If the tribunal finds the dismissal to be unfair, it can order:

- reinstatement to the same job; or,

- re-engagement to a different job; or,

- compensation

Most employees seek compensation and even if they have asked for reinstatement or re-engagement, industrial tribunals may be reluctant to order this remedy if the relationship between the employer and employee has broken down.

COMPENSATION

Compensation consists of:

- a basic award

- a compensatory award

and in some circumstances

- an additional award

- a special award

BASIC AWARD

The basic award is calculated as in redundancy, but with no minimum age limit. There is an upper limit to the amount of weekly pay which has to be taken into account and this is reviewed by the government each year. Reckonable service to be taken into account when calculating the basic award is limited to 20 years.

COMPENSATORY AWARD

The compensatory award takes account of financial loss, including future earnings, as a result of the dismissal and lost benefits including loss of pension rights. The maximum award which can be made is reviewed by government each year. There is no maximum award when the unfair dismissal is the result of sex, race or disability discrimination.

REDUCTION OF AWARDS

Both the basic and compensatory awards can be reduced to take into account the extent to which the employee contributed to his/her own dismissal.

ADDITIONAL AWARD

This award is made if the tribunal issues a reinstatement or re-engagement order and the company fails to comply with it. The tribunal may then make an additional award of between 13 and 26 weeks' pay, subject to the same weekly maximum limit as the basic award.

If the reason for dismissal was sex, race or disability discrimination, then the tribunal may order a higher additional award of between 26 and 52 weeks' pay.

SPECIAL AWARD

Special awards are made to employees who have been unfairly dismissed on account of their trade union membership (or non-membership) or trade union activities, and have asked for reinstatement. In these cases a minimum basic award is payable, based on a figure set by government each year.

If the tribunal decides not to order reinstatement it can order a special award of one week's pay × 104 – more if the maximum figure set by the government is greater.

If reinstatement is ordered but not complied with, the amount of the special award is one week's pay × 156 or a figure set by government, whichever is the greater. There is no upper limit on the weekly pay figure in this case.

CONSEQUENCES OF UNFAIR DISMISSAL

To lose an unfair dismissal case can be extremely costly, particularly in times of high unemployment, when future loss is taken into account. The applicant (ex-employee) has a duty to mitigate his/her loss by seeking other employment but this may not be easy to come by and the compensatory award will reflect this.

Win or lose, going to tribunal is very costly to the employer even if the company decides to present the case itself and not employ legal representation. The time taken in getting the facts, putting the case together, preparing the "bundle" (documents used to support the case), deciding which witnesses to call, not to mention the day or days actually spent at the tribunal, represents a substantial wage bill.

Tribunals are therefore to be avoided if at all possible. This should, wherever possible, be done by prevention. To settle all unfair dismissal claims out of court in order to avoid going to tribunal, whatever the circumstances, sends the wrong signal to employees who may perceive it as a way of getting money out of the company. If the case is perceived to be good then the company will probably defend it. Whether they win or not will depend on the extent to which they have acted reasonably and followed their own disciplinary procedure.

BIBLIOGRAPHY

Training Your Staff Bambrough, J (1993) The Industrial Society
Evaluation of Training Reeves, M (1993) The Industrial Society
Discipline, Grievance & Dismissal Morris S (1993) The Industrial Society
Statutory Matenity Pay Morris, S (1995) The Industrial Society
Sensitive Issues In The Workplace Morris, S (1994) The Industrial Society

For a complete list of Industrial Society publications please contact
The Industrial Society
48 Bryanston Square
London Will 7LN
Tel 0171 262 2401